Praise for *The Dance of Leadership*

"*The Dance of Leadership* frames the issue of leadership in a new and insightful way. It's a cliché to say that leadership is an art, but the Denhardts actually demonstrate not only why it's art, but also how one can apply the principles of artistic performance to improve individual and organizational leadership. This is powerful and timely stuff."

—Roger Hughes
Executive Director, St. Luke's Health Initiatives

"Using concepts and experiences drawn from the arts, this book makes an elegant and persuasive case for a new language of leadership, one quite different from traditional command and control models in favor of an art of leadership that engages and energizes people and causes them to act. Modern leaders will resonate with the Denhardts' description of leadership; those seeking to become leaders would be well advised to do so as well."

—Lattie F. Coor
President Emeritus, Arizona State University

"*The Dance of Leadership* shakes up conventional wisdom about management. Just when you think nothing new can be said about leadership, the Denhardts come along with an innovative interpretation full of fresh ideas and valuable insights."

—Jay Hakes
Executive Director, Jimmy Carter Presidential Library

"We can talk about leadership as an art and not a science, but Bob and Janet Denhardt go beyond talk. They take us to the heartbeat of leadership itself. *The Dance of Leadership* evokes the artist within each of us in a way that makes leadership natural and accessible to all."

—James Keene
Executive Director,
California State Association of Counties

"Bob and Janet Denhardt have added a new dimension to the leadership 'industry'. *The Dance of Leadership* provides energy to all leaders who are brave enough to learn that leadership is most of all an art that has to be discovered together with the people they are leading."

—Jan Sturesson
Global Leader, Big Cities Network,
and Partner, PricewaterhouseCoopers

"Leaders, like dancers, rely on their passion, intuition, and discipline to refine their craft and connect with their followers. This premise is the core of the highly original perspective on leaders and leadership presented in *The Dance of Leadership*. Through conceptual presentations and examples, Bob and Janet Denhardt encourage the novice to learn the craft from masters and the master to refine and improve his or her art by exploring that of others. The innovative perspective makes the book a 'must read' for all aspiring and experienced leaders who want to touch deep-seated emotions in their followers and energize them into action."

—Afsaneh Nahavandi
Director, University College,
Arizona State University, West Campus

The Dance of Leadership

The Art of Leading in Business, Government, and Society

Robert B. Denhardt and Janet V. Denhardt

M.E.Sharpe
Armonk, New York
London, England

Library of Congress Cataloging-in-Publication Data

Denhardt, Robert B.
The dance of leadership : the art of leading in business, government, and society / by Robert B. Denhardt and Janet V. Denhardt.
p. cm.
Includes bibliographical references and index.
ISBN 0-7656-1733-1 (cloth : alk. paper) — ISBN 0-7656-1734-X (pbk. : alk. paper)
1. Leadership. I. Denhardt, Janet Vinzant. II. Title.

HM1261.D46 2006
303.3′4—dc22 2005024993

Printed in the United States of America

The paper used in this publication meets the minimum requirements of American National Standard for Information Sciences Permanence of Paper for Printed Library Materials, ANSI Z 39.48-1984.

BM (c) 10 9 8 7 6 5 4 3 2 1
BM (p) 10 9 8 7 6 5 4 3 2 1

Speak to the animal in us
And the animal will answer.
Speak to the human in us
And a voice in song will rise.

Alberto Rios

CONTENTS

PREFACE

The Dance of Leadership is about understanding leadership not as a science but as an art. Here we bring together the experiences of artists, musicians, and especially dancers, on the one hand, and leaders in business, government, and society, on the other, to clarify the artistic elements of leadership. The result is a new way of thinking about leadership, a new language for describing the act of leading. When leadership is exercised, groups and organizations are given purpose and direction, and people are "energized"—their lives take on new emotional meaning and their interpretation of the world shifts, sometimes imperceptibly, sometimes dramatically. And that is an art, not a science.

The lessons contained here can be employed by anyone who aspires to lead, at any level. They apply to leadership in families, in small groups, in clubs, in large organizations, even in whole societies. For some these ideas will come naturally. For others, more work will be required. In either case, these ideas will provide a new focus on what leadership is about and will enable all of us to work more consciously on building our leadership skills. Like other arts, the art of leadership resists explanation, but it can be made more clear and accessible to those who wish to practice it.

In the development of these ideas, we have been helped and supported by an important group of friends and colleagues. We want to give special thanks to Vesna and Louie Ajic, Jess Alberts, Maria Aristigueta, David Baker, Dick Bowers, Terri Brower, John Bryson, John Byrne, Heather Campbell, Kelly Campbell, Russ Cargo, Tom Catlaw, Linda Chapin, Howard and Marilyn Coble, Don Coons, Bob Cunningham, Craig and Lisa Curtis, Cyndi and Don Cutler, Mary Ellen Dalton, Peter and Linda deLeon, Michael Denhardt, Michael Diamond, Tom Downs, Suzanne Fallender,

Frieda Friedli, Mark Glaser, Guy Gordon, Mary Ellen Guy, Jay Hakes, John Hall, Tom Hulst, John Jacko, Phil Jeffress, Ed Jennings, Colleen Jennings-Roggensack, Jennifer Kaufman, Jim Keene, Brian Marson, Barbara McCabe, Craig McGregor, Cynthia McSwain, Tony Montoya, John Nalbandian, Sandra Parkes, Alex Pattakos, Laura Peck, Phil Penland, Jack Pfister, Gerald and Marcia Pops, Jeff Raffel, Jay Roundy, Frances Salas, Faye Schmidt, Anne Schneider, Phil and Hannah Schorr, Ron Scott, Ed Sheridan, Billy Siegenfeld, Jan Sturesson, Lisa Takata, Ed Twardy, Marty Vanacour, Orion White, Bob Wingenroth, and Ann Zinn. Special thanks go to our editor and friend Harry Briggs for his faith and encouragement in this project from its beginning.

We also deeply appreciate the time we spent with those we interviewed and those we have worked with in *The Dance of Leadership Workshop*. By convention, we note without citation where we have drawn quoted material from our interviews, and a list of interviewees is contained here as an appendix. We have also drawn on the experiences of many workshop participants, though we have chosen to fictionalize their stories, which appear scattered throughout the text. The wonderful insights that all these people have provided are the raw material from which this book has been constructed. We deeply appreciate their contribution to the dance!

Bob and Janet Denhardt
Santa Barbara, California

The Dance of Leadership

1

Exploring the Art of Leadership

A corporate executive describes his job as finding the speed to take his company around the corners just on the edge, "right before we go off the cliff, not slower, not faster."

A member of a work team waits until just the right time to make her suggestion and, in capturing the moment, activates and energizes the group.

A college basketball coach acknowledges that he is doing his best coaching when all he has to do is sit there and watch his team play.

A little girl on a playground skips and dances and twirls from group to group. As she does so, the rhythm of each group changes to match her own.

Each of these people, from the corporate executive to the little girl on the playground, is leading. But they are also taking part in a dance. They are moving expressively and rhythmically, leaping into the future with confidence and imagination. They are acting based on intuition and empathy, relying on their "feel" for the situation. And they are fully in the moment, completely present to what is happening here and now. Leaders like these excel because they can sense what is around them, because they have practiced their craft, and because they trust themselves and others enough to modify and improvise their steps as they go. They are engaged in the dance of leadership.

If you listen to leaders talk about what they do, they will tell you that there is at least a significant part of leadership that relies on forces that can't be explained in rational or scientific terms. That's why so many leaders say, "Leadership is an art, not a science." There is an aspect of leadership that remains a mystery. There is that "special something" that some people seem to have, either innately or by training and experience, that sets them apart. But no one seems to be able to tell us how to prepare for and build this more "artistic" side of leadership.

In this book, we take seriously the notion that leadership is an art and we explore some of the ways people in business, government, nonprofits, and other organizations develop the artistic side of their leadership. If leadership is an art, then one way to learn about leadership and especially about how leadership might be developed is to study the more traditional arts, to see how people in those disciplines approach their work, and then to apply those lessons to the art of leading.

That was our approach here. We began by first learning as much as we could about art, music, and especially dance, then conducting a series of in-depth interviews with some of this country's premier artists, especially dancers and choreographers—people such as David Parsons, whose Parsons Dance Company is one of the leading exponents of modern dance; Liz Lerman, whose Liz Lerman Dance Exchange has brought dance together with civic dialogue for Americans of all ages, races, and interests; and Septime Webre, artistic director of the Washington Ballet and one of the truly "cutting edge" choreographers in contemporary ballet.

From these artists, and many others, we learned about some of the elements that artists, musicians, and dancers consider as they construct their art. We learned about the importance of space, time, and energy in shaping the human experience, we learned about the many and varying rhythms of human interaction, we learned about the importance of images and symbols in communicating human emotions, we learned about improvising with creativity and spontaneity, and we learned about the importance of focus, passion, and discipline in a performance and indeed a career.

Perhaps most important we learned that artists, musicians, and dancers clearly believe that these artistic elements can be taught or at least improved upon. While leaders might say that "timing is everything" or realize that much of their work is actually "improvised," artists not only understand these ideas, but they have developed approaches and strategies for *learning* the skills applicable to these problems. Art, even the art of leadership, can be developed, and those in the more traditional arts can provide excellent advice on how to go about that.

Having learned some of the lessons that the arts hold for leadership, we turned back to the world of actual leaders and asked how these ideas might apply. In some ways the parallels were obvious, as in the examples of "timing" and "improvisation." But beyond that, thinking of leading in terms of art gave us new insight into what leaders do and how their skills might be improved. In order to test these ideas, we conducted in-depth interviews with a number of important and thoughtful leaders in business, government, nonprofit organizations, the military, higher education, and the world of sports. These interviews included people such as George Fisher, who was chairman and CEO at Kodak and previously CEO at Motorola; Jane Hull, the first woman to serve as Speaker of the House of Representatives in Arizona and later secretary of state and then governor; and Phil Fulmer, who guided the Tennessee Volunteers football team to a national championship in 1998 and was recognized by the Football Writer's Association as the national "Coach of the Year." With these leaders, and many others, we talked about the artistic side of leadership and discovered that many of the ideas we had drawn from the arts did indeed resonate with their experience and, in many cases, caused them to understand that experience in new and more textured ways. Most important, they helped us develop new ways of thinking about how the skills of leadership might be taught and learned more effectively. In this book, we will use the words of these artists and leaders to convey some central ideas about the art of leadership.

In the remainder of Chapter 1 we will explore more fully how we see the connection between art, music, and especially dance, on the one hand, and leadership, on the other. We will also outline a new way of viewing leadership, one drawn directly from the arts. In Chapter 2, we examine some of the lessons that this new perspective suggests, starting with the idea that artists see the world in a way quite different from others, that they see the world in terms of an especially intense and textured interplay of space, time, and energy that brings special context and dynamism to the work they do. In the chapters that follow we explore the more specific lessons we can draw about the dance of leadership, ideas such as the rhythms of human interaction, including the important notion of timing (Chapter 3), working with images, symbols, and metaphors, especially in interpersonal communications (Chapter 4), improvising with creativity and spontaneity (Chapter 5), and the importance of focus, passion, and discipline in art and leadership (Chapter 6). In the final chapter (Chapter 7), we consider how thinking of leadership as an art can assist in the development of leadership skills.

What Is the Art of Leadership?

Consider the experience of Ron Bennett. Ron worked for many years as an executive with a company making household appliances, such as washers and dryers. He directed a research and development unit, most recently working on computer-controlled dispensing of detergent based on how dirty the clothes are. Ron came to observe over the years that while some of the managers of his division were more successful than others, the successful ones didn't always use the same style or approach. One of the most beloved and successful managers had been Chris Ramsey. Chris was gregarious and warm, and made people in the whole division feel a sense of camaraderie that had not existed before. He was enthusiastic and always ready to offer words of support, encouragement, and congratulations for a job well done. Although Chris had been promoted to the corporate office a year earlier, staff still talked about what a genuinely caring person he was and how he somehow made them feel important and want to do their very best.

But the new "boss," someone who had been brought in from the outside after Chris left, was quite different. From his first day on the job, Phillip Hornback almost seemed to be the opposite of Chris. He was more dignified than warm, and a bit of an introvert. His reputation was as an honest and honorable man, and he showed himself to be respectful of others' ideas. But he was quiet and tended to watch and listen rather than lead discussions at staff meetings. Although he was never unkind, when he did speak he was matter-of-fact, task oriented, and focused on setting and achieving short- and long-term goals.

Ron at first found this approach unsettling, and was concerned about how other people were reacting to such a different leadership style. He asked several of his longtime friends in the division what they thought. Somewhat to his surprise, they were very positive. Laura Evans, whom Ron considered one of the most thoughtful people in the division, felt that it was "about time" that someone came focused on accomplishing tasks and setting and achieving ambitious goals. "Someone needs to focus on goal setting and performance measures and make sure that we're getting the work done." After all, she said, "If we can't show a consistent profit, we're all going to be looking for jobs somewhere else. And we're all way too old for that!" More importantly, she said, "he seems like a good, decent man. I trust him."

Likewise, Jim Jacobs, Ron's closest friend, seemed to have a favorable impression of his new boss. "You know, Phillip's style is not what we are used to," Jim told Ron, "but I completely respect him. He really has some good ideas about how we can improve the work we do here. And his technical expertise is just superb. I've never seen a nonscientist that knows washing chemistry better. He's helping me to be better at what I do. He's going to put us out front, you know."

Ron mulled over his friends' comments. How could two such different leaders inspire trust and confidence among the same people doing the same work?

Many people say that they don't know anything about art, but they know what they like. The same could be said of leadership. Most people would be hard pressed to define good leadership, but they know it when it's there and they miss it when it's not. In the case of both art and leadership, different individuals react differently. One person may respond quite enthusiastically to a painting or a piece of music while another may find it atrocious. A particular approach to leadership may deeply move one person while it leaves another flat. To the untrained eye, it may seem entirely subjective. But the more you know about either art or leadership, the more you are able to discern differences between good and bad, profound and trite, inspiring and boring.

Good leadership, like art, touches us. It stimulates not just our minds, but our emotions, and makes us come alive. Certainly we expect that leadership will help us to accomplish things we might not otherwise accomplish, and so we look for results. But leadership also touches us in more personal ways. Good leadership excites and activates us. Good leadership inspires and encourages us (that is, it gives us courage). Good leadership makes us feel better about ourselves. It is this emotional side of leadership that provides the energy to move and to change small groups, large organizations, and even whole societies.

Leadership is about change, moving people in new directions, realizing a new vision, or simply doing things differently and better. Change, in turn, involves deeply rooted human values. These are the ideas and commitments—about oneself, about others, and about one's work—that people cling to based on faith and conviction. It is in large measure because of these values that significant change is almost always accompanied by emotional turmoil.

Put simply, people are attached to their values. When people choose to follow another with energy and resolve, when they commit to engage in a shared effort to transform a group, an organization, a community, or a society, they do so based on an emotional connection, a faith in something better, a belief that the change is both well thought out but also consistent with their own ideals and values. We may go along with monetary incentives, management reports, and performance targets, but only leadership that touches our emotions and is consistent with our values will engage our full energy. Real leadership speaks to matters that express deeply seated feelings, emotions, and indeed, basic human values.

Since the world of art speaks in the language of feeling and intuition, it's not surprising that many leaders have considered leadership an art. For example, Max De Pree, chairman emeritus of Herman Miller, Inc., draws an analogy between the leader of a jazz group and a leader in industry. In this view, leaders are seen as rarely able to write and conduct a "symphony" that others play. More often, they are called on to be fully integrated into the performance themselves, to play along with others, like the leader of a jazz ensemble improvising: "By establishing the theme, the leader of the ensemble . . . can chart the basic pattern and direction in which the performance will move. By setting the tone and the tempo, the leader gives focus to the spirit and energy of the group. By modeling effective and responsible performance in their own solos, leaders can energize and articulate the performance of others. But it is the performance of others that is critical."

Similarly, a number of writers on management have at least alluded to the connection between leadership and art. For example, management theorists James Kouzes and Barry Posner write that "Leadership is a performing art . . . [in which leaders] *enact* the meaning of the organization in every decision they make and in every step they take toward the future they envision." In much the same way, professors Lee Bolman and Terrence Deal argue that managers who would lead in the future will require high levels of personal artistry to respond to the ambiguous and paradoxical changes they will face: "Artists interpret experience and express it in forms that can be felt and understood, and appreciated by others. Art allows for emotion, subtlety, ambiguity."

Though there are a few references to the parallels between art and leadership in the management literature, even these are typically brief and passing metaphors, acknowledgments that some leadership skills are difficult to describe in rational terms. And while several writers examine certain approaches or behaviors that are rightfully described as artful, at least in the sense that they can't be explained scientifically, the art of leadership has not been developed in any detail. Moreover, these works fall short of suggesting that leadership may share even more with art than the simple metaphor of leadership as an art might suggest. Our position, to the contrary, is that if leadership is an art, then there may be much to be learned about leadership by asking how those in the visual arts, music, and especially dance approach their disciplines, and then by translating that material back into the world of leadership.

In addition, we want to focus specifically on leadership and not management. We want to understand the act of leading wherever it occurs, but since leadership and management are so easily confused, we need to begin by distinguishing between the two. Management, we would say, is concerned with rational processes that largely operate within a given space and time, while leadership is concerned with more intuitive processes that move beyond the existing limits of space and time. Management works within a world of order and regulation, while leadership works within a world of openness and change.

But the matter is more than a little confusing because there is some overlap between these terms. We want managers to lead. And we recognize that leaders often engage in behaviors that are more like management than leadership. It helps if we think about leadership not as a particular role in a group or organization but as a function or activity that many people engage in from moment to moment and day to day. We tend to think of leaders as those "at the top," those in formal positions of power and responsibility. But leadership can also be viewed as a specific type of action, so that we can distinguish between the act of managing and the act of leading. What is it that people do when they are leading? What is distinctive about leading as a human activity? We think that the essential element of leading is the effect this activity has on others, specifically the fact that leadership energizes other people. (We'll explore this definition in more detail later.)

We find leadership of this type highly artistic. Leadership, like art, rarely involves algebra, calculus, or analytic geometry. There's no scientific answer to the most difficult problems that leaders face, and those problems are not amenable to solutions sought through the application of rational analytic techniques. In both art and leadership there is always incomplete information and, indeed, that's a central part of the problem. If there were complete information, then perhaps we could apply scientific techniques. But information is never complete. Leaders, like artists, have to move from moment to moment, trying one thing and then another until a path reveals itself and they can move on. The cubist painter and poet Georges Braque once wrote, "In art there is only one thing that counts: the thing you can't explain." One might also say that the only thing that really counts in leadership is that which you can't explain.

The difference between management and leadership is quite similar to the difference between science and art. Indeed, some have said that the artistic dimension of leadership is exactly what distinguishes it from management. When you draw up lists of personality traits of good leaders, such as honesty, credibility, intellect, insight, strong communications skills, and so forth, you find that those lists contain many items that apply to managers as well as leaders (indeed, all that we just mentioned do). But if you identify those tasks that leaders undertake and the skills that they need beyond those of managers, these are the items that associate most easily with art. They have to do with perspective, intuition, rhythm, timing, and developing a sense of the situation. Business executive Chester Barnard put it well many years ago when he wrote that, for executives, the essential skill is "the sensing of the organization as a whole and the total situation relevant to it. It transcends the capacity of merely intellectual methods, and the techniques of discriminating the factors of the situation. The terms pertinent to it are 'feeling,' 'judgment,' 'sense,' 'proportion,' 'balance,' 'appropriateness.' It is a matter of art rather than science, and it is aesthetic rather than logical."

At its core, leadership is an art, not a science. Without art, leadership is bound to only those solutions that rational analysis and managerial control can provide. Without art, leadership is merely management. Regardless of the context in which one works, from church groups to small businesses, to nonprofit organizations, to large corporations, to communities, to the military, and to the top levels of government, more than management is needed from our leaders. It's not surprising, then, to find the following definition of leadership from one of the most significant public leaders of our time, former secretary of state Colin Powell: *"Leadership is the art of accomplishing more than the science of management says is possible."*

Drawing Lessons from the Arts

Raul Martinez almost got it. Raul had served since the early eighties as vice president for corporate giving for a major health care products firm. He considered himself someone who was deeply engaged in the community and he thoroughly enjoyed being able to guide corporate investments so that community groups would benefit. Consequently, he often found himself at cultural events, ranging from community arts performances to the Pennsylvania

Ballet. He also considered himself a student of leadership. After all, he was in a position from which he could watch major corporate leaders interact not only with people inside the company, but also with people at all levels in government, in nonprofits, and in the business world.

One night, while watching a particularly outstanding performance by a local jazz dance group, Raul suddenly recognized that what the dancers were doing was the same thing he tried to do at work. The dancers were trying to connect with the audience, to draw them into the music and the dance. They were trying to build an emotional connection with people in the audience that would energize and excite them. When the dancers succeeded, they seemed to then draw on that energy from the audience and build on it. And, Raul reflected, that's exactly what leaders do. He thought, "If only we could bottle the energy that's on that stage tonight and take it into the corporate world." But it was a passing thought, one that would have been considered a little "on the edge" back at the office and one he didn't even recall the next day.

What is it that the arts have to say that is really relevant to leadership? This is the question we asked as we began this book. As we have said, our thinking was that if leadership is an art, then it only makes sense for those interested in leadership to draw upon other artistic disciplines. There are many artistic fields in which there is a long and substantial intellectual tradition and in which devices for training those entering the field have been well worked out. That's why we have schools of art, schools of music, and schools of dance. People in the world of art understand what art is all about and they regularly develop the artistry of aspiring painters, musicians, and dancers. Maybe they know something that those of us interested in leadership don't.

We began by learning as much as we could about art, music, and especially dance, and by talking with some of the most notable figures in those fields. We wanted to learn how they approach their work and how their ideas and approaches might help in studying and learning the skills of leadership. What we found was striking. Not only are art and leadership closely parallel; in many cases they seem indistinguishable. Take, for example, the following quotation: "We must be willing to take risks, committed to the experience, and ready to be vulnerable and open to the self-discovery that is a natural product of the process. We must be willing to listen to others and to be generous with them. An active balance of self-fulfillment and response to others' needs has to be maintained. Basically we need the courage of our own impulses and responses qualified only by a healthy concern for the people we are working with." While we might easily assume that this quotation came from an important leader or a best-selling book on leadership, in fact the quotation comes from an introductory text in dance!

The dramatic similarity of those lessons being taught in schools of dance and those we find essential to leadership suggests that the parallel between art and leadership is extraordinarily compelling. This conclusion was reinforced as we talked with dancers, choreographers, and artistic directors working with major dance companies. While we draw lessons from all the arts here, we focus in this book primarily on dance and choreography. Why do we think these fields might prove particularly helpful in generating lessons about leadership?

First, dance takes place in a moment in time, then the moment and the dance are gone forever. Unlike painting, in which the artistic products are available for people to see at any time, dance, like music, is fleeting. The performance occurs and then it's over, left resident only in your memory. Dance is, in many ways, an illusion. It's not something you can hold in your hand. It's not something that you can touch. It's not something that you can smell. It's not something you can come back to and revisit the next day or the one after. But, the irony is, as choreographers Lynne Blom and Tarin Chaplin point out, "to create the illusion, you need the reality of the articulate human body, sweating and thumping along."

Leadership is, of course, very much the same. The act of leading is not something that can be captured and preserved, even in these days of digital cameras and streaming video. Leadership occurs in a moment and then it is gone. As Walter Sorrell puts it so eloquently and in a way that speaks to leaders as well as dancers, "Life only lasts the very moment of our awareness of it, and all that remains is, as in the dance, the memory we can retain of it." For the leader to touch someone's emotions, something must happen in an instant. For that moment, there must be some sort of connection, a shared experience, a shared meaning, a shared emotion.

But then the moment is gone and another appears. So, like dance, leadership is illusory, fleeting, momentary, fragile. And yet it needs the physical actions of the leader to make it happen. There is something about the reality of the leader's tone, the leader's speaking, the gesture, the inflection, or another of a million subtle cues that "connects" with others and compels them to follow. And it has to happen in a moment or it won't happen at all.

Second, dancers and choreographers have to work within a certain structure, the structure of a particular time and a particular place, and with the interaction of many people (which itself imposes structure). There is a great deal of creativity that is involved in dance, yet that creativity occurs within the context of relatively specific structures. Septime Webre, artistic director of the Washington Ballet, told us that because those in dance have "to marry a high degree of structure and discipline with great creativity, we [in dance] can view the world in ways that accept structure. There's a certain amount of structure that's set and I believe the world is healthier because of that. A society that has structure and order provides for freedom. It provides for and fosters creativity." Note that other artistic disciplines are less constrained by structure than dance; for example, a visual artist who works alone may be less concerned about the interaction of his art with that of others. But note also that Webre's comment was that structure actually spurs creativity.

Obviously, leaders work within the limits of particular structures as well. For the leader, those structures include the groups or organizations or communities within which the leader acts. The leader is bound by the history of those involved, their established patterns of interaction, and their expectations about appropriate leadership behaviors. It makes a difference to the leader whether people in the group or organization "go way back" together. It makes a difference what their values and beliefs are. It makes a difference what they think about the person who would lead, whether it is someone coming from the outside or someone who has been there all along. These conditions structure what leaders can do. And yet they also contain elements of freedom, little openings into which the leader can move to offer insight, support, and direction.

Third, like the other arts, dance is, to a great extent, a skill-based discipline, though, as we will see, one supported by significant personal resources. Just as the painter needs to know the proper brush stroke and the musician needs to be able to sustain a smooth vibrato, the dancer must learn endless sequences of positions and movements. Dance is not just an intellectual enterprise and it can't be learned in more than a rudimentary way just by reading books or watching other dancers. Dancers must acquire specific skills through a combination of instruction, practice, and psychological discipline.

It's more unusual to talk of leadership as a skill-based discipline, but that's exactly what it is. There are certain skills that leaders employ. There are things that leaders do that cause others to follow. Many who lead actually employ these skills without conscious preparation, and indeed they often wonder why others perceive them as leaders. A major corporate figure recently told us, "people are always coming up to me and complimenting me on my leadership. But I don't really know what I'm doing. It's just natural to me." This is probably one of those cases where some of the skills of leadership are simply "built in."

For others, leadership may not come so naturally. But the skills of leadership, especially those associated with the art of leadership, can be more clearly defined and developed over time. To do so, of course, does not involve merely reading biographies of famous leaders or watching other leaders in action. Rather, just like learning dance, learning the skills of leadership requires a combination of instruction, practice, and psychological discipline. But it is clearly possible to improve one's leadership skills. So in answer to the classic question about whether leaders are born or made, we would say "both"—that is, some skills seem natural to some people, other skills have to be developed through learning and reflection, and sometimes simply through time and experience.

There are a number of reasons to suggest that learning more about how artists, musicians, and especially dancers approach their work can aid in understanding the world of leadership. Both dance and leadership combine deep personal commitment and insight with specific skills to help us bring the future into focus. Both work within specific structures, but do so with an eye toward deriving the greatest possible creativity from the context within which they occur. Both ultimately aim at establishing a sense of moving forward together. As one critic remarked, "When you boil it all down, that is the social purpose of art: the creation of mutuality, the passage from feeling into shared meaning." And, we would say, that's the purpose of leadership as well—achieving shared meaning.

A New Language for Leadership

People tend to think of universities as being a little more open and responsive than other institutions, but they certainly have their share of hierarchy and top-down leadership, just like other places. That's why Jeff Rich, a young faculty member in political science, found his new dean, Mary Augustine, so remarkable. Not only was Mary always open and engaging at a personal level, but as a leader she seemed to be steps ahead of others. Mary just seemed to have a special talent for engaging others and aiming their work in the most positive directions.

While Mary had good ideas herself about modernizing the curriculum and about how to attract more and better students, her real skill was in bringing people together to discuss such topics fully and completely, then guiding them to consensus. Her approach was not to plant ideas, and certainly not to manipulate the group, but rather to try to discover what each person felt and where the group would find common ground. "It's amazing," she once told Jeff, "how these people come up with such good ideas, ideas that are much better than any I might have come along with. You just have to release the right energy and things go in amazing directions."

Jeff was especially impressed at how Mary had the capacity to take a number of good and often very complex ideas and boil them down to a few statements that seemed so simple but captured everything that the group had said. She had the capacity to capture just the essential elements, but, in doing so, made the ideas accessible to everyone in the group and to those outside. Finally, Jeff observed, Mary was able to move the group to act, at just the right time and with just the right momentum. As Jeff watched her in action, Mary never seemed to be "in charge," at least not in the old-fashioned top-down way, yet she was undoubtedly one of the very best leaders Jeff had ever seen.

As we noted earlier, we are interested in identifying exactly what leaders do that causes other people to follow. For this reason, we are interested in the act of leading as opposed to what those in formal positions of leadership do. There are two reasons for this view. First, we think that leading is something that people do at all levels of society and in all areas of human endeavor. Some lead more formally and more often than others, but all are capable of leading and in fact do so from time to time. Second, even those in formal positions of leadership engage in a variety of activities, some of which involve leading, some of which involve management, some of which involve other things. We are interested in identifying some of the essential elements that distinguish the act of leading from other human activities.

We recently heard someone who had coached Olympic athletes point out that while different basketball players or different golfers seem to shoot the ball or swing the club in different ways, those differences are largely differences of personality. An engineer studying the basic human motions involved in the shot or the swing would point out certain elements of speed, torque, and acceleration that are indispensable to the success of the shot or the swing. The essentials stay the same even though the personalities differ. Similarly, while leaders may appear to be different based on their personalities and the situations they find themselves in, there are certain essentials that they share, often without even knowing it. They do certain things that cause others to think of them as leaders, and to follow. While the personalities of leaders make different leaders seem quite different, there are essential skills that all possess.

What is it, then, that is distinctive about the act of leading? What is it that causes others to become vitalized and begin to move in a new direction? Our answer is that the essence of leadership its is capacity to "energize," for the leader to touch and to move people, to animate them in pursuit of a better future, one in which problems are solved, one in which progress toward important goals is made, and one in which the human condition is improved. In part, this can be done as the leader works with others to come up with good ideas about how things should be done and then communicates in a way that people find objectively convincing. (Note that while "coming up" with good ideas might be something the leader does alone, it is increasingly more likely a matter of the leader assimilating and integrating the good ideas of many others.)

But even generating good ideas is rarely enough. In order to energize others, even in the pursuit of objectively "good ideas," the leader must connect with them at a more personal level. As we said earlier, people can get interested in explanations and justifications, but they are rarely "energized" without some kind of an emotional commitment. For this to happen, the leader must trigger, stimulate, or evoke an emotional response on the part of potential followers so that those people will become engaged and active. Only when people are "moved" emotionally will they begin to "move" psychologically and physically.

The capacity to energize others through touching the emotions is the key to the art of leadership. To the extent that we can learn how leaders make that emotional connection, we will improve our capacity to lead at whatever level we find ourselves. We can enhance our understanding of the art of leadership by looking at other artistic disciplines, because in all its variations, art aims at arousing or inducing feelings such as pleasure, pain, joy, anger, tenderness, elation, shock, fear, or wonder. By learning about the artistry of emotional connection, we are able to identify the "essentials" of leadership and to suggest ways in which individuals at all levels can increase their capacity for leadership.

The act of leading involves shaping and giving direction to the energy that individuals have and the energy that is constantly exchanged between and among people. This energy is the "raw material" of artistic leadership, and understanding and working with and through the rhythms of social energy is an essential leadership skill. The best leaders have a special sensitivity to the shifting rhythms of human emotions. And they have a special talent to touch and move people and groups at a very basic level. The actions that these leaders take and the expressions they make trigger a certain emotional response in others, people who are then much more likely to be "energized" around whatever issue they face. Leaders are in the business of shaping and giving direction to human energy as it flows through space and time.

Obviously, such a view of leadership is quite different from the traditional view of leadership as giving orders or creating structures for control. Perhaps that is what leadership once was, but no longer. Looking back, we can outline the traditional tasks of leadership, the old "job description" of the leader, as follows: the leader's role is (1) to come up with good ideas about the direction the group or organization or society should take, (2) to decide on a course of action or a goal to be accomplished, and (3) to exert his or her influence or control in moving the group in that direction.

But this "job description" no longer works. While perhaps suited to the formal leader of decades past, this view simply doesn't fit circumstances today. No one individual can be expected to come up with all the best ideas about where the group or organization should be going. Moreover, having one individual decide on a course of action not only limits the options available, but also limits the commitment of the others to the course chosen. And, if anything, asserting excessive power or control in trying to move a group is likely to backfire over the long term. Most people don't want to be told what to do; they want to be a part of what is being decided and undertaken.

In contrast to this traditional view of the leader's role, leadership today is exercised by one who: (1) helps the group or organization or society understand its needs and its potential, (2) integrates and articulates the group's vision, and (3) acts as a "trigger" or stimulus for group action. This view recognizes that all members of the group have aspirations not only for themselves but for the groups and organizations and communities and societies of which they are a part. Involving many people in assessing the potential of the group, then constructing an image of the future together, is both more effective in the long run and morally the right thing to do. The leader's role is to bring the group together, to facilitate its discussion of future possibilities, and to provide an initial "push" to get things moving.

The leader should aid in creating an open and visible process through which members of the group can express their needs and interests and in which the leader helps maintain the integrity of the group process and a dedication to the group's vision. This is not at all to say that the leader must just sit back and wait for the group to act, for the process of bringing forward ideas, stating them in terms that are meaningful to people, and communicating them in a way that resonates with people throughout a group, organization, or society is extremely hard work, indeed, much harder work than simply trying to control people. But it's also much more likely to result in a clear direction and sustained energy on the part of the group.

Think, for example, of the way things happen when a small group is brought together to address a problem or complete a task. Often the conversation will swirl around inconclusively for a while (sometimes a long time) until one person makes a suggestion that others pick up on and begin to act upon. People's reactions may be based on the substance of what was said or on the way in which it was presented or, most likely, some combination of both. But, in any case, we would say that where people react with energy and enthusiasm, leadership has been exercised, or, to say it in a different way, an act of leading has occurred. The act of leading need not have been an act of the formal "leader" of the group, even if there is one, but leadership has still occurred. So you can think of leadership retrospectively: when you see that a group has been energized, you can say that an act of leadership is likely to have just occurred. In cases such as this, what's critical is not a scientific approach, but the artistry of the leader.

Reprise

So what is it that leaders do, consciously or unconsciously, that causes others to follow? We think the answer lies not in the leader's providing explanations, but in the leader's connecting with people in a way that energizes them and causes them to act. The leader must touch not only the "head" but also the "heart." The leader must address basic human values and do so in terms of the future. What distinguishes the act of leading from other human activities is that the leader makes an emotional connection with others around issues of personal values and energizes them to move in a new direction. As we said earlier, leadership energizes.

But leadership also provides meaning. The world of art is one in which artists, musicians, and dancers help us sort out the complexity and the meaning of our lives. The philosopher Suzanne Langer writes, "A dance . . . expresses the nature of human feeling—the rhythms and connections, crises and breaks, the complexity and richness of what is sometimes called man's 'inner life,' the stream of direct experience, life as it feels to the living. . . ." Certainly we should expect no less from leadership. We should expect and in fact demand that leadership help us to confront both our dreams and our demons, to comprehend our most exalted moments and those in which we fail to live up to our best, and to give us strength to express our inner being. To engage in and to respond to this kind of leadership, we will suggest, is to enter into the dance of leadership.

2

The Interplay of Space, Time, and Energy

An executive, sensing that where she sits in a crowded meeting will make a difference in the way people respond to her, moves instinctively toward the "head" of the table.

The chief of staff to a gubernatorial candidate comments over and over that, in politics, as in life, "timing is everything."

A community arts activist recognizes the difference between her style and that of a friend by saying "I'm go, go, go and she's oooooh so slow."

The chief executive officer of a hospital walks through the wards and senses the almost palpable shifts in energy as he moves from one part of the hospital to another.

To oversimplify, there are two ways of relating to others, through the head or through the heart. We can appeal to logic and reason, explaining our ideas in the most precise and objective terms, hoping that the other will understand our argument and find it persuasive. Or we can try to connect through the emotions, by sharing a part of ourselves in a way that we hope will touch the other's feelings and trigger some hidden interest, perhaps even excitement. Both are valuable.

Unfortunately, the modern world has steered a little too far in the direction of the intellect. It has sought to rationalize and to quantify what may be neither rational nor quantifiable. Consistent with this general tendency, many have come to accept a rather narrow "managerial" view of leadership, one that focuses our attention on "plans," "resources," and "outputs," as opposed to questions of human emotions and human values. Leaders have increasingly been defined as those who can move the organization toward its stated goals and objectives, that is, leaders have been seen as concerned with the details of managerial processes affecting the bottom line.

In contrast, real and enduring leadership is an emotional, intellectual, physical, and even aesthetic experience that involves our heads, our hearts, our fundamental selves. Leadership is not just a matter of "what we do," but "who we are." The world of "what we do" is concerned with attaining given goals in the most efficient way possible. In that realm, the old language of "command and control" doesn't seem completely out of place, especially as it is expressed in more contemporary and more subtle terms such as "motivation" and "empowerment." The world of "what we do" is concerned with getting people to do what we think is necessary in order to accomplish what we want to accomplish.

The world of "who we are" is different. It centers on developing our human potential, with our having the capacity and opportunity to be all that we can be. That, of course, involves individual choice. People must have the chance to make decisions about those things that are important to them and then to choose how best to achieve their individual and very personal goals. The world of "who we are" is played out in our relationships with other individuals as we work together in small groups, as we participate in social, civic, and religious organizations, as we enter the world of work, and as we understand our roles as citizens.

Dancers and choreographers, like other artists, speak to the world of "who we are." They are concerned with getting things done efficiently, but they are more concerned with establishing an emotional connection or bond with others. They don't think just in terms of objects or inputs, but in terms of symbols and metaphors, the currency of the emotional world. When the dancer looks at the "field" that is being presented, he or she thinks in terms of *space* and *time* and *energy*, time being the sequence and duration of events, space being their relation to one another, and energy being the motive force that provides the spark of power and imagination, creativity and spontaneity, liveliness and imagination that causes people to respond.

These elements of the dancer's world make considerable sense for leaders as well. Though they would rarely use these words, leaders also operate in a world of space, time, and energy. Thinking about leadership in these terms permits the leader or potential leader to see his or her "field" in a new and valuable way. In this chapter, we explore the three categories suggested by the world of dance: space, time, and energy. In each case, we say something about the dancer's perspective, but also demonstrate the implications of such a perspective for leadership. Following our survey here of some *perspectives* that dancers and leaders might share, we move in later chapters to a discussion of some specific *skills* as well as certain *inner resources* that the world of dance suggests for the world of leadership.

The Elements of Dance

At a recent workshop, we discussed the ways in which different leaders think about and move through their days. Emily Scales began the discussion by talking about her calendar and how tightly her calendar bound her actions during the day. "If it's not on my calendar, I don't do it," she said. "I come into my office in the morning and I pretty much know what the day will be like. And there's not a lot of flexibility. I'm booked pretty tight so that if someone wants to see me I just ask them to contact my assistant for an appointment." Wayne Collins looked sympathetic. His day, he reported, was not so much bound by appointments as by "things to do." He told us that he had attended a time management seminar some years ago and now religiously keeps lists of "things to do" and carefully programs each day so that the most important tasks are sure to be completed. When we asked Emily and Wayne how they *felt* about their days, both responded that everything seemed programmed and mechanical. "Everything is so structured," Wayne said, "that I sometimes lose a sense of the importance of what I'm doing, you know, why I'm doing it. I just move through the day with no sense of what it's all about. It's like Mark Twain said about history—it's just one damn thing after the other!"

Otis Taylor then joined in the discussion, saying that he understood how much pressure people feel today to get things done as quickly and efficiently as possible. But, he said, "You have to have some 'flow time' as well." When we asked what he meant by "flow time," he told us that he felt it was necessary to preserve some time each day in which he could "flow" from place to place and person to person, not just moving from appointment to appointment or from task to task, but allowing times and spaces for genuine human interaction. "I have to stay in touch with my people in a personal way. If I don't, I start to lose them. In fact, I also start to lose myself. Having a little cushion built into my day so that I can occasionally just go with the flow is very important to me. That's the only way I can sense the energy and enthusiasm of those I'm working with and the only way they can see mine. It's very important." Most in the group thought Otis really had hit on something, but when we talked about how to put the idea into practice, most came up with dozens of reasons why finding "flow time" in their organizations would be difficult. As we left the room, Otis said quietly to one of us, "Don't they know that's the most important thing leaders do?"

Artists generally are concerned with conveying emotional content that resonates with their audiences, whether in the theater, in a gallery, or on a street corner. Dancers and choreographers go about that task by manipulating symbols and metaphors through patterns of movement, often accompanied by music. In order to make their work meaningful, in order for them to touch those who are watching and engage their attention and appreciation, they must work with staging, music, lighting, costumes, set design, and many other aspects of the performance. But most important is the *perspective* that dancers and choreographers bring to their work. *Artists see the world differently from other people*. Anna Deveare Smith, a theater artist and playwright, commented, "The value of the artist is in the mind that sees things differently from a civil rights lawyer." It's as if there are different lenses for viewing the world and artists have a lens at their disposal that is unfamiliar to many others.

Managers, for example, see the world from an "organizational" viewpoint, that is, in terms of the manipulation of resources to produce goods or services. Lawyers see the world from a "juridical" viewpoint, that is, in terms of contested issues waiting to be fought out in courtroom settings. Dancers and choreographers see the world in terms of a different set of elements, each absolutely critical to the expressing and communicating of human emotion. These elements are space, time, and energy. These fundamental ideas or structures, highlighted by the artistic "lens," initially form the backdrop or "canvas" upon which the dancer or choreographer pursues his or her art, but they also become the tools the artist manipulates through imagination, through creativity, through abstraction, through design, and through performance.

Human activity, whether dance or leadership, has to be organized so that it flows through time and through space with a certain level of energy or intensity, but also with a certain degree of freedom and release. Without attention to space, time, and energy, creating that flow would be impossible. But with the right combination of these elements, with everything coming together in just the right way, people move through time and space at an appropriate rhythm, expressing the energy they feel and transferring that energy to others. We think that leaders or potential leaders would benefit from thinking in similar terms and, indeed, based on our interviews, we would say that the best leaders already do so. They just use different words to describe their experiences.

There's really nothing mysterious about these elements. We are all bound by them, but, for most of us, our attention is elsewhere. Liz Lerman, founder of the Liz Lerman Dance Exchange, shared with us the following example: "On the most simplistic level, I think about how I choreograph my way out of the house in the morning, especially when my husband and I each try to get out of the house at the same time with the child 'intact.' I used to laugh because it was much easier for me. It felt choreographic, because you even sequenced what you put on your back. Then you finally get out the door and you didn't forget anything." That's probably a familiar scene for many readers, but most probably don't think of it in terms of choreographic categories such as content or sequencing or time, as Liz Lerman does. Yet once you begin to think in those categories, they help you better understand what's at play in that example.

There are, of course, many other ways in which we move with energy through space and time. We get out of bed and get dressed in the morning, activities situated in certain spaces and taking a certain amount of time, which by force of habit we can estimate fairly well. If we work in a building downtown, we either drive to work or take public transportation, now moving through much larger measures of space and at a distinctly different and faster pace. As we travel along, we may encounter traffic or experience overcrowding on the bus or train, either of which may disrupt our expectations about the time it will take to get downtown or what we think of as our appropriate allocation of space, our "territory." We don't want to be slowed down and we don't want people pressing too close. It throws off our sense of time and space.

We arrive at work and enter our office, a clearly defined space in which we undertake various activities during the course of the next several hours. We may also move to different spaces, such as a conference room, and experience a different spatial or temporal dynamic. Similarly, throughout the day, we may perform some activities with strong passion and intensity, while at other times we are fairly passive and reactive. We may also notice that our level of activity or passivity may not be matched by others. Some topics for which we have great enthusiasm seem to bore others. And vice versa. We experience the world in terms of space, time, and energy, but still we rarely think in those terms, especially when we talk about leadership.

Not only artists, but also the best leaders, seem to have a better sense of the flow of space, time, and energy than others, and those who would like to improve their leadership skills can do so in part by giving greater attention to these elements. For now we should simply be reminded that groups, organizations, and societies move through time and space with greater or lesser degrees of energy, just as individuals do. Think of a basketball team going through the course of a game. The players' actions are bounded by a specific space and a specific time—the court and the time-clock—but these are merely backdrops against which the players, individually and as a squad, structure bursts of energy that flow through the more specific time and space. One of the important roles of the leader is to organize the flow of energy through time and space so as to best achieve valued results.

Consider the United States's 1960s ambition to put a man on the moon. In 1961, President John Kennedy told Congress, "I believe that this nation should commit itself to achieving the goal, before this decade is out, of landing a man on the moon and returning him safely to the Earth." President Kennedy's expression of that goal had the effect of restructuring the way we thought about space and time, both in the sense of how we understood distances and travel times between the earth and the moon, and how we might structure our political and organizational time over the next several years. Moreover, because people responded to the emotional challenge that the president presented, much greater social and political "energy" was focused on the space program. We would say that the primary effect of the president's leadership was to put in motion or to "trigger" certain activities undertaken through a newly energized sense of time and space, and entered into by those in NASA as well as people throughout the nation.

In the remainder of this chapter we will explore each of the three elements of dance: space, time, and energy. In each case, we will take a quick look at how dancers and choreographers approach that element, but focus on some of the ways that leaders might benefit by greater attention to that way of thinking about human action. Again, it may make most sense to think in terms of lenses. Looking through one set of lenses we see certain things; looking through another set of lenses we see different things. Our question will ultimately be whether our skills in leadership can be enhanced by at least occasionally adopting a set of lenses that help us see space, time, and energy a little more clearly.

Working with Space

Anyone who occasionally watches sports recognizes that some players "see" the court or the field in an almost uncanny, but more complete way than most. Basketball players like Michael Jordan, John Stockton, or Allen Iverson have a special "feel" for what's going on all around them, not just what's immediately in front of them. They know where all their teammates are, they know where the opposition players are, and they know just where to position themselves to best take advantage of that distribution of players on the court.

Sometimes it's as if they are watching the movement or the "flow" of the game from up above, able to see everything at once.

It's certainly possible to draw sketches of the court on chalkboard, and, of course, coaches do that all the time. You can see where the X's and the O's are most likely to line up and where the offensive players might be repositioned, for example, to take advantage of a particular defensive alignment. But the game, of course, is never that static. The coach may anticipate some situations, but in the flow of the game, things always happen that are completely unpredictable (in fact, that's probably what we enjoy about the game). Yet when that unpredictability comes into play, the great players seem to understand just what is happening. They see the whole "field" and they react accordingly. Leading a fast break, they know when to drive, when to veer out, when to pass off and then "spot up." And sometimes, driving toward the basket, they flip the ball directly behind to a trailing player better positioned to go to the basket. They couldn't have seen the player behind them, and, with the noise of the crowd, they probably couldn't have even heard the other. But because they could see the whole "field," they knew someone was there and that the other player was in a better position to score.

Leaders, especially those who lead large and complex organizations, are perhaps most familiar with the concept of space as a way of ordering human action. We recognize that many of our activities take place in buildings or other fairly defined spaces. We recognize the subtle differences in attitude and approach that accompany the move from one space to another. We feel better, more alive, in some buildings than we do in others. We know that seating arrangements in a conference room or other meeting space have some significance. It makes a difference whether people are seated around a long rectangular table with someone clearly at the head of the table or whether they are seated around a circular table with no discernible "power" position. And we are quite familiar with the spatial depiction of our businesses and agencies in organizational charts. These are all familiar and important ways in which space affects the work we do.

Dancers and choreographers extend this understanding of space by recognizing that space is something that both affects and is affected by emotional or feeling content. To start with, dancers recognize the dynamic interaction that occurs between and among physical bodies moving in space. Whatever one body does in space affects what others do as well. Jean-Louis Barrault, the well-known French actor and mime, made the point that everyone is connected: "The mime must first of all be aware of this boundless contact with things. There is no insulating layer of air between the man and the outside world. Any man who moves about causes ripples in the ambient world in the same way a fish does when it moves in the water." It's like a human "butterfly effect."

Some have even argued that we are constantly giving off subtle signals with respect to movement in space and that those signals we send out and those we receive shape our movement behavior. For example, imagine looking from above at a crowded intersection with dozens of people on either side of the street waiting to cross. The light turns green and people start toward one another, yet remarkably few bump into anyone. There seems to be some hidden "guidance" system in operation. People seem to be constantly giving and receiving directions as they move.

Dancers and choreographers are, of course, interested in the effect that the movement of people in space has in terms of emotion. There are a variety of ways in which dancers and choreographers discuss space; the terms include level, shape, direction, dimension, perspective, and focus. But just for purposes of illustration, think for a moment about what is communicated by someone lying down or staying close to the ground, or, alternatively, someone beginning to rise and ultimately standing, or, again, someone leaping high in the air. The body in the low position is likely to convey rest, gravity, or simply being deeply "grounded." The body in the standing position has more options, more freedom, and can change direction or speed easily. The leaping body, at least in our culture, conveys joy, exhilaration, or transformation.

Of course, it gets even more complicated when you add other dancers. For example, a balanced or symmetrical placement of dancers on the stage, say, in two rows on either side, gives the impression of stability and calm, whereas an unbalanced or asymmetrical arrangement implies movement or dynamism. The way that an individual occupies a space is important, but what becomes even more important are the *relationships* among the various dancers, the pattern that they form and how they move vis-à-vis one another. It's not the individual bodies that the choreographer is working with, but the relationships among them. Dance educator Victoria Hutchinson captured this point by telling us that "When you play around with space and play around with time, it's really the *relationship* of those bodies that's the most interesting." It's the capacity to understand the impact of various patterns or shapes that is the key to successful choreography.

For most leaders, and certainly for most managers, there is a tendency to think of space in fairly rigid terms. We understand the idea of space, but typically we focus on space without movement through time. Such a static view of space is familiar to those working in complex organizations, for whom the organizational chart is the ultimate spatial representation of how the organization is supposed to operate. (It's comparable, of course, to the coach's chalkboard mentioned above.) But, of course, what is completely missing from the chart is any sense of movement through time, any variation in focus or balance or flow, any dynamism. For the leader, having a capacity for design, for patterning, and for developing relationships is absolutely essential.

The patterns that must be grasped by the leader are largely built around human relationships. While most of the management literature focuses on the manager's interaction with one person or with small groups, the leader needs to see not just individuals but overall patterns of relationships. Those, after all, may ultimately be what is most important in moving forward. To be able to see and understand relationships the potential leader must have a special sense of pattern or design, he or she must be able to see not just the "dots," but ways of "connecting the dots." Obviously, there are endless combinations of relationships that can be employed by leaders, especially as you begin to think in terms of "sculpting" human energy in space. For our purposes here, one important aspect of leadership is the capacity to visualize the space within which human energy moves and help give shape and direction to that energy.

Being able to see the whole "field," as we said before, is a very special capability of the most effective leaders. As we said, some athletes, such as Martina Navratilova and Wayne Gretzky, seem to have a "sense " for the game that derives from knowing where everything is and where everything is going. Hockey legend Gretzky, for example, is supposed to have said, "Others skate to where the puck is; I skate to where the puck is going to be." Most leadership occurs in settings other than athletic fields, though certainly some occurs there. But it's appropriate to speak of leaders generally as needing to recognize all the components of a situation that are in play at any particular moment and to have a sense of spatial relationships so as to know what to expect next. The leader needs to be able to "skate" to where the action is going to be, not just where it is. Whatever the setting for leadership, leaders benefit from being able to see the whole field, and that's a matter of recognizing and working with patterns in space.

The key is the leader's capacity to see movement, pattern, and design in the flow of human energy. As we have said before, for some people the capacity to see design in their everyday living is quite natural, even taken for granted. For example, bringing together a multitude of ideas and concepts generated through endless conversations and reports, then sorting out the essential and doing away with the trivial, is an absolutely critical leadership skill. Indeed, many who use this capacity in leading may not even recognize that this is what they are doing. For others that capability needs to be consciously developed; it needs to be constantly recognized and nurtured over time.

The leader's capacity to understand the flow of human energy through space and time is clearly related to the much more embracing capacity to recognize the relationships and patterns that hold life and lives together. Some leaders, some artists, even some philosophers, have special capabilities in this regard. It is their creativity with respect to seeing and understanding these patterns and relationships that constitutes their greatest creative ability. "There are certain underlying orderly arrangements in everything beyond and within us. More than the inventing of new things, creativity often implies the discovery of these underlying orderly arrangements." Leaders who are able to grasp the "underlying orderly arrangements" that hold human beings together will have a special advantage.

It's not at all easy. These arrangements are often complex, overlapping, and seemingly random; some appear as patterns only over the long term and, for that reason, it's easy to miss them. But the leader, like the artist, must have the special ability to see and understand patterns or relationships, then to employ that understanding in a singular fashion. From the morass of ideas and information that characterizes life today, the leader finds, isolates, and then highlights significant patterns. Leaders, more than others, excel in recognizing and recovering form, sorting out the relevant elements of shape and space from those that detract, and identifying patterns in relationships that others fail to see. Indeed, we might say that even beyond the leader's creativity in solving problems or coming up with new "visions" for the group or organization, the leader's most creative skill is that of finding significance in the patterns or flow of human relationships.

Working with Time

Statement: "Time flies." Response: "I can't. Their flight is too irregular." When one of the author's elementary school teachers returned from a linguistics convention to share with her class the joke that had been the "buzz" of the whole meeting, her young students first struggled to figure out the joke, then groaned at how bad it was. But, after many years, we're coming to recognize that there's an even deeper layer of meaning in the puzzler. The flight of time itself is irregular. That's something that Jim Meredith, CEO of a major corporation, helped us learn.

Jim was reminiscing about how strange and unpredictable his path through life had been. He was a math and physics whiz in high school and was clearly destined for a career in the sciences. Indeed, he went to graduate school in mathematics and ultimately received a doctorate from the University of Texas. The direction of his life and his career seemed to be laid out clearly in front of him with a steady progression of contributions, perhaps one day leading to a Nobel Prize. After only a few years in a very prominent research and development lab, however, he became manager of the lab. Suddenly his career had shifted. He was no longer a mathematician, he was a manager, something completely foreign to his experience. But he adapted well to his new role and, again to his surprise, was soon asked to move to a substantial position in the financial management area. Now his work was still in part managerial, but also financial. But he adapted well and eventually moved on to the top executive level in his company, eventually becoming its chief executive officer, responsible for all aspects of the business.

Jim marveled at how this had come about. His career certainly could not have been predicted from anything that happened early on or at least anything that was apparent early on. There was certainly no "straight arrow" of movement through time and career. Yet in retrospect, maybe there was: What held all these different jobs together was the fact that Jim had somehow developed a love for business. He just lived and dreamed business all day and often into the night. But he never would have guessed that early on. And even if in high school or college he had thought that one day he would like to be CEO (which he never did), he wouldn't have had the slightest idea how to direct his career to that end. Rather he just did what he enjoyed and went along for the ride.

Certainly, he speculated, other people may have driving ambitions that propel them through life toward a single goal. "But my experience is that a lot of people like that 'crash and burn' along the way. They are just too obsessed, too intense, and they just don't enjoy it." There's also a lesson in this for the way top leaders view time, he continued. Lots of managers have strategic plans with long-term objectives laid out and lots of boxes and charts making it appear that the company's development simply involves moving from one box to the next. "But the real genius of leadership is to think more broadly, to see the full expanse of time and opportunity, to recognize the openings that present themselves for the company to grow and expand, and to be ready to move, sometimes on a moment's notice. It's not linear, it's not mechanical, and it's not step-by-step. It's the ability to see today how you are going to look back on things twenty or twenty-five years from now."

In what we have called the science of leadership, time is rarely given any real attention, and is certainly not seen as the complex, dynamic, vital, intense, powerful flowing, sustaining, but ultimately mysterious force that we know it to be. We are amazed daily at what time brings, at how "time slips away," how "time flies," and how "time is money." In organizations, however, we rarely talk explicitly about time, except for two important exceptions: when we talk about efficiency and when we talk about planning. When we talk about efficiency, we are not only concerned with a relationship between inputs and outputs, we are concerned with the time and energy expended in completing tasks. This was, of course, the basis for the classic "time and motion" studies, studies that continue to have a familiar ring. When most people talk about planning, it's usually to consider the future and how we can move successfully into the future. But even here, when we talk about time, what we do is to "spatialize" time, that is, to convert time into space, such as when we construct something like a PERT (Program Evaluation Review Technique) chart or a strategic plan.

Too often these efforts result in a set of categories, each assigned a space or a temporal "box," with the assumption, as Jim Meredith noted, that if we move steadily from box to box, we will have success. Of course, what is missing is that time doesn't "stand still" as we move through those boxes. Other things are happening around us and if we fail to live in "real time" our plans will immediately become outdated, "relics" having little relevance to our new present. That's probably why so many strategic plans wind up permanently housed on a distant shelf.

We will consider the dual issues of rhythm and timing in the next chapter, so our discussion of time in this section will be limited. However, it is important to say a few words about the way we experience time and the way we structure time. The anthropologist Edward Hall provides an excellent starting point. For Hall, time constitutes an invisible language that people employ in their own activities and in their interactions with others. But it is a language that varies from culture to culture and indeed from group to group and organization to organization.

Hall lists two ways of thinking about time, the first being *monochronic time*, a typically Western view in which events are scheduled as separate items, one at a time. Within this concept of time, activities are largely conducted in accordance with a schedule that allows us to concentrate on one thing at a time and to "manage" our time, so as to allocate our temporal "resources" in a way that reflects our priorities. Those things that are most important are granted larger chunks of time. The alternative, *polychronic time,* involves people doing many things simultaneously, as in a Mediterranean marketplace in which crowds gather clamoring for service but there is no apparent order to who will be served next. The shopkeeper attends to many customers at the same time.

Hall argues that each of these times has advantages and disadvantages. Thinking of the world in segmented monochronic compartments may be helpful in dealing with linear tasks, but of doubtful value in dealing with nonlinear or creative activities. Such an orientation can actually alienate people from one another and reduce their attentiveness to the context, the world around them. Polychronic time, on the other hand, can involve many people at once, but with so much interaction that those accustomed to another mode of time might wonder how anything ever gets done. In organizational terms we might think of these differences as the result of different leadership styles, but remember, Hall is talking about cultural differences in the way we conceive of time.

Dance, of course, depends on a polychronic view of time, an orientation toward time that allows many things to be happening at once. Two dancers at the front of the stage are moving at a moderate tempo but beginning to recede, all the while creating powerful visual images. At the same time, three other dancers toward the back are moving at different speeds and in different directions. There's a lot happening at once, but what's most important is the overall impression. And, to make matters more complicated, the choreographer has to design each individual moment, but then organize the flow of all the separate moments into a complete production.

Septime Webre of the Washington Ballet spoke to us about the tension between the individual moment and the entire creation in this way: "You have to orchestrate the moment. The composer takes noise and organizes it in music. A choreographer takes chaos and organizes a moment. And orchestrating the moment is more than just rhythm or technique. It's those and more. I think in terms of going rapidly through time. Orchestrating the moment, then seeing in advance in an abstract way how long is needed to make it work." And, of course, making it work means making it touch the audience, a process that is neither mechanical nor contrived, but one that is dynamic and changing.

Two members of the Department of Dance at Arizona State University, Claudia Murphey and Mila Parrish, talked with us about how they teach choreography. Students are given problems or scenarios to work out in movement, then their efforts are critiqued and they start again, trying something new to see if it works better. The course is based on problem solving, finding solutions, and recognizing that there are multiple solutions to any problem. In that sense, Murphey suggested that the course "becomes a metaphor for life. You have to allow yourself multiple solutions to a problem. You have to get to the point where you are not willing to be stopped in your tracks. If there's a roadblock, try to be creative and find a way around it. That life skill is worth everything."

But because the choreographer works in polychronic time, things are always changing and consequently the solutions change from moment to moment. The choreographer isn't working with a set of finite objects, but the ever-shifting, evolving relationships among people. Parrish reflected, "In the process of making a work, new possibilities arise, new potential solutions. The playing field is open, is active, is alive, is responsive." The choreographic design is never a progression from box to box; rather, it's a swirling mix of bodies in motion, of symbols and meanings that float in and out, of music, of colors, and of time mixing with space in the most unpredictable ways.

Leaders, we would suggest, also need to break away from the bounds of structured, mechanical time and the finite boundaries it sets. Yet unfortunately, this is exactly the concept of time that we most often use in organizational settings, where we seek ways of ordering the supply of time so as to achieve organizational objectives in the most efficient way possible. Among the problems leaders encounter, one of the most difficult has to do with bringing the right people or objects to the right place at the right time. A related issue is raised by the fact that certain actions must follow others in a prescribed order. Finally, the frequency with which events occur is an issue. What's important to note is that all these questions are usually treated within the framework of monochronic, linear, mechanical time. Remember that while that view of time seems to predominate in modern organizational life, it is not the only one available.

We said earlier that leaders need to think outside the spatial boxes we construct for ourselves. But leaders also need to think outside the normal temporal boxes as well, to entertain the limitless possibilities that time and circumstances allow, and to give motion to activities that will flow together toward an uncertain but hopefully better future. Alcine Wiltz, chair of the Department of Dance at the University of Maryland, told us, "Time gives you a referencing point. Maybe it's like a canvas out there with all these little points on it. It's finding the right connections of the dots. There is something that's alive in front of you and . . . you are constantly putting it in some structure." Structure in this sense is not the type of rigid confine that limits or constrains; instead, it might be better equated with "form" or "order" or even "statement," in the sense of "making a statement." (A dictionary definition of "structure" doesn't contain the idea of rigidity or containment that we ordinarily associate with that term; rather, it has to do simply with the interrelation or arrangement of parts in some complex fashion.) For the leader, structures are not there to constrain, but rather to provide for free thinking. One executive told us: "I'm someone who really wants to be able to make changes until the time that changes can't be made. That's difficult for people who think in a more linear way."

While managers may be able to think in terms of moving from one box to another, the flow of human energy that leadership activates is never just such a movement. Rather, in the process of leading, new possibilities arise, new potential solutions. The leader's field, like that of the dancer, is open, active, and responsive. It sometimes involves a maddening mix of bodies and personalities, of ideas and images, or projects and proposals, all coming together in the most unpredictable way. When all these forces crystallize in perfect action, in harmony with one another, there is a sense of "flow." Things feel right and people feel good.

Leaders inevitably deal with the future and with movement through time, that is, they deal with change. For this reason, a leader's understanding of time must always incorporate far more flexibility and openness than that of others. The leader has to psychologically entertain more than the immediate moment or the one that follows. This is not to say merely that the leader is a futurist or "star gazer," but rather that the leader has to embrace the fact that people and events flow through time and that the flow of time, the flight of time, is irregular. Embracing that fact in turn means that the leader must be especially adept at sensing the changes that time brings (or allows) and shaping the flow of human energy through time. And again, it is not a matter of imposing limits. The notion of flow implies a certain degree of freedom and release as well. The leader well attuned to issues of time will be able to shape the flow of energy but also to allow others to figure out for themselves how they can best "go with the flow."

What can the leader learn from the arts about time? We found the following quotation helpful. While the words deal with art, as you read the quotation, simply substitute "leadership" for "the arts," and "leader-like" for "artistic." You should find the lessons for leadership remarkably on target.

> The arts give practice in using trial and error to get something right; relying on one's senses, intuition, and critical judgment to make creative choices and decisions; understanding how images and other nonverbal modalities are used both literally and metaphorically to create meaning; holding several possibilities in awareness and being open to change; recognizing that there are many ways of getting from here to there and that (unlike in spelling, arithmetic, grammar, or computer programming) there is more than one solution to a problem. Making artistic connections and seeing aesthetic relationships gives experience with solving complex problems and understanding systems in a variety of contexts. Through the arts, one learns that many problems (such as important life decisions) have no clear-cut method for solution but that an awareness and exploration of possibilities is the first step in addressing them.

From the arts we learn that creativity and structure can coexist, that structure can even promote greater creativity. What's ultimately most important for the leader, however, is not the structure but the ever-changing space inside the structure, because that's where the subtleties of evolving human relationships unfold. Therein lies the freedom structure provides, but that's not something we can see in a linear, mechanical way. Time provides the possibility for transformation, but only if we first transform time.

Working with Energy

Anne Petron was head of Investment Banking and Claude LeClair was head of Global Asset Management for a major financial management firm specializing in investment banking and wealth management for an international clientele largely based in Europe. Both were considered not merely strong managers but real leaders in their firm and in their industry. But there was a dramatic contrast in how they approached their jobs. Anne was a bundle of energy, always moving about, always laughing and engaging others, always "on." People marveled at how she could physically go from early morning to late at night seven days a week, but also at how her excitement for her work was always front and center. When someone asked about this, she responded that "The excitement that I show for our work carries over to everyone else here. Besides, I draw energy, indeed strength, from everyone here that I interact with. It's really a mutual thing."

Claude was a real contrast. He was considerably more subdued, and markedly slower and more deliberate in his speech and movement. He exuded a quiet and calm confidence that seemed to affect others he worked with. There was nothing showy in the way he went about his work. Yet people reacted to his positive outlook, his steady spirit, his assurance, and his unshakeable determination. In his part of the firm, there was a widely shared attitude that nothing was too big or too difficult to handle and that, when presented with a problem, people would simply go about solving it, quickly and quietly. As they did for Anne, people had enormous respect for Claude and would follow him anywhere. When asked about the difference between Anne and himself, Claude responded, "Actually we're very much alike. While our personalities are different, we both give off energy to those around us and take in energy from them. We just do it in different ways. But that energy is what keeps us and our organizations going."

Dancers talk a lot about energy. There's the energy that flows from inside and supports the physical movement. There's the energy that's exchanged between people. And there's a general sense of energy that sustains the creative process. The master of movement notation, Rudolf Laban, could have been speaking of any of these variations of energy when he described "the inner impulse from which movement originates." Energy, meaning effort, force, quality, or vitality in action, is triggered by something inside, then revealed in the outside world as pattern or example. Dance instructor Constance Schrader puts it nicely: "What inner impulse moves a lion when stalking its prey? What inner impulse moves a puppy to chase a ball? What inner impulse moves an ant to follow other ants in collecting food? Effort in dance concerns the skills of discovering and presenting the muscular, mental, and emotional state that shows the inner impulse or essence of the dancer's subject."

Energy is not just that which moves the body and leads to sweat and sore muscles. Rather, energy is expression, the coming together of time and space, pattern and purpose, so that an inner intention is translated into external action, sometimes involving one person, but typically involving many. Merce Cunningham, award-winning choreographer and artistic director of the Merce Cunningham Dance Company, once wrote, "Dance provides something—an amplification of energy—that is not provided in any other way, and that's what interests me." Energy is something that permeates everything that dancers do. In our conversation with him, Robert de Warren, artistic director of the Sarasota Ballet, even placed energy at the center of personality: "Obviously a personality is an energy that emerges from the person." It is an expression of who we are.

People are constantly giving off energy and constantly receiving energy from others. Recall what we said about positively connecting with others at an emotional level, not just with the head but with the heart. Sometimes the heart that is affected is your own, as when you are awakened by the creative spirit. Ann Halprin, director of the San Francisco Dancer's Workshop, commented: "I'm very excited about dance and love it with a deep passion. I also struggle, tire and become discouraged. But what has always revived me . . . has been the rebirth of energy each time the creative process is awakened and artistic activity begins to unfold even in some infinitesimal measure."

At other times, energy is expressed in a relationship, not simply as a metaphor, but as something that is real. Robert Shields, America's greatest mime, and perhaps best remembered as part of television's Shields and Yarnell, told us that the audience is a source of energy: "I completely work off their energy. It's never just me on stage. It's me with them. The whole show is about them. The audience has a tremendous rhythm, and just a little energy goes a long way—it only takes a few people to get it going." Similarly, Matthew Neenan of the Phrenic New Ballet in Philadelphia remarked, "You have to let the audience's energy come into you."

Just as dancers are concerned with energy and speak in terms of drawing forth energy, building energy, exchanging energy, and renewing energy, so might leaders benefit from thinking in these terms. The energy, the expression of the leader, like that of the artist, comes from a number of somewhat surprising sources, among them our orientation toward the future, our capacity to draw excellence from inside, and our pursuit of beauty or human value. It plays out in several different ways. First, energy orients us to the future. Dance is never solely historical, even when it is set in the past. Rather, the lessons that dance teaches, like the lessons of any art, are almost always forward looking. Dance, at its best, touches us in deeply human ways, leaving us with ways of seeing the world that perhaps we lacked before. We go to the theater to experience emotions we might not otherwise experience, and we take away from that experience new ways of facing the future.

Surely the same is true of leaders, whose primary concern is the transition between the present and the future. This is not to say that leaders need to see the future and direct the rest of us in that way. Rather, they must have the capacity to reveal our yearnings and our passions (even when we are unaware of them), and then to turn these into aspirations for the future. For any leader, at whatever level, the act of leading involves a relationship between present and future. The world of those who lead is inherently one in which the leaders are living "on the edge," the edge of the present as it falls into the future. Pauline Koner, dancer, choreographer, teacher, and writer, put it this way: "The person who only mirrors his period is not doing what an artist should do: act as a catalyst in society. If he sees only what is, he is not transcending the immediate. The artist must ask: 'How does one challenge this? How does one make life meaningful?'"

Second, the dancer, the leader, or, more generally, the creative individual has a commitment to expressing his or her inner life and a dedication to revealing that inner life in some external form. The artist draws on the outer world for both insight and inspiration, but ultimately it's what's inside that really counts. Margaret H'Doubler, perhaps best known as a dance educator, once wrote, "Any work of art, to be significant and convincing, should grow from what its creator has within, growing and changing as the germ idea changes." The artist draws from deep inside to isolate some essential aspect of life and bring it to our awareness so that we give it our full consideration. In our conversation, David Parsons, founder of The Parsons Dance Company, put it this way, "You see the essence of life—or what should be the essence of life."

Similarly, the leader draws from the outside world; indeed, the capacity to draw from the outside world is fundamental. Yet the leader also has to dig deep into his or her own consciousness (or even beneath consciousness) to draw forth a new interpretation, a new formulation, a new twist on the way people have been viewing the world. Leading requires sensing both what's going on in the outside world and also what's happening inside oneself, then shaping that inner experience in a way that will resonate with those in the outside world. Almost paradoxically, it's only through this personal immersion that the leader can articulate the vision of the group or organization. Leadership requires bringing forward the best that's in you and along the way revealing the depths of your inner life in a very public way. We agree with psychologist George Hagman that leadership, like art, does not merely capture how we feel: "It articulates who we are, a living person with an inner life with its rhythms and connections, crises and breaks, complexity and richness." Of course, this is also the ground for growth and creative development.

Third, the energy of dance is an energy directed toward the creation of beauty in the world. If we think about leadership in these terms, certainly it produces effects in the personal and social world. Where leadership is present people do things differently, they engage in different patterns of action, and they aspire to different visions. But are the acts of leaders oriented toward creating something of beauty? Certainly when we think of art, we typically think of objects of beauty or at least those things that we find attractive, in the sense that we are drawn to them because they somehow speak to us. We believe that leadership relies on a similar frame of mind, not necessarily one oriented toward beauty per se, but one open to exploring new configurations of *human values*. In the world of leadership, the art is not increasing beauty in the world, but increasing the capacity for the realization of significant human values. In this sense, the "frame of mind" of the leader is one that is open to insight, to revelation, to greater clarity.

Reprise

Does it make sense to speak of leadership in terms of time, space, and energy? Certainly dancers think so, with one remarking that in an improvised dance, "if there is a leader, it will be shown by distinctions of space, time, or energy." But most leaders also sense that the groups and institutions within which they work are marked by displays of energy moving through time and space. In many situations, you can walk in the door of a company or a city government, let's say, and immediately sense the atmosphere, the spirit, and the tone of the organization. Marshall Dimock, an early leader in the field of public administration, remarked, "Having studied the relation of bureaucracy to enterprise all of my adult life, I have no doubt that institutions appear to have personality, vitality, and self-perpetuating qualities. There is also no doubt that these institutions quickly disappear when whatever produced these energies in the first place also disappears." There is no question that the elements of time, space, and energy are at play in groups and organizations and societies. The only question is whether leaders will see them.

3

Understanding the Rhythms of Human Interaction

Two people are walking down the street together. One ordinarily walks faster and the other slower, but they adapt their pace to their mutual walk. They also accept a common rhythm in their speech—who says what, when, and how often.

An astronaut preparing for a night launch spends several days in advance adapting his patterns of sleep to the need to be well rested in the early evening.

An executive notices that by slowing the pace and intensity of her work, she gains considerably in terms of the quality of the work—and the quality of work life.

A military commander who wants to find just the right time to send a strike force into enemy territory waits an extra day and misses the opportunity.

Artists of all types, but especially musicians and dancers, often talk about rhythm. Leaders rarely do so. However, rhythm is at the core of human life, a gateway to the emotional experience of individuals, and, for that reason, rhythm is central to the experience of leadership. From the steady beat of our hearts to the clicks of our keyboards, from the cycles of our sleep to the pace of our work, rhythm forms the framework of our experience. As choreographer Matthew Neenan pointed out when we asked about rhythm, "Even in a lawyer's conference room, there's a definite dance going on among the people who are speaking and voicing their opinions. There's a definite rhythm." Success in leadership is dependent on the leader's recognizing, understanding, and engaging the rhythms of human interaction. A key element of the leader's capacity to influence the emotional tenor of a group is the capacity to understand and to shape the group's rhythm. To be able to grasp the rhythmic structure of a group or organization and to understand the complexities of rhythms as they interact with one another allows the leader to see beneath the surface and to penetrate the superficial elements that draw our immediate attention, but may be largely irrelevant to the underlying movement of the group.

The leader who is able to integrate the often divergent rhythmic patterns of groups or organizations will be able to move the group forward in remarkable ways. The leader's ability to exercise good timing, to see when the rhythmic pattern of events provides just the right opportunity to bring forward a proposal or to bring together just the right people, dramatically enhances his or her capacity to energize the group. Most important, having a good sense of the rhythmic dynamics of human interaction permits the leader to see "openings" through which a group, an organization, or even a society can move. For many who lead, a good sense of rhythm and timing seems "built in," simply a part of their makeup. For others, learning more about rhythm and more about timing, and then actively applying that new understanding in day-to-day situations, will enable and support surprising new acts of leadership.

All of us innately understand rhythm, at least at a subconscious level. Developing a more conscious awareness of rhythm is what allows us to use rhythm to move ourselves and others forward and to gain a better sense of timing. Consider what is involved in rhythm and how rhythm connects to the important question of human emotions. We are perhaps most familiar with rhythm in a musical sense, and within music, we are probably most familiar with rhythm in metric terms, rhythm as a steady, even, consistent, recurring pulse, the "beat" of the music. We recognize that musical rhythms may vary, especially in terms of the "pace" or the speed at which the beats occur. Even if we don't know the musical terms, we can easily understand the difference between *adagio*, a slow, easy, lyrical tempo, and *allegro*, a quick, lively, spirited tempo. We also can understand the differences in complexity found in different rhythmic patterns, such as the difference between the fairly straightforward and uncomplicated (though often very fast-paced) rhythm that characterizes bluegrass music or most rock and hip-hop, and the more complex rhythm of a drum line in a marching band or a jazz tune such as the Dave Brubeck's classic "Take Five."

But rhythm doesn't just refer to a steady beat continued indefinitely. Some rhythms come in phases or cycles, such as the natural phases of day and night or those of the four seasons. Those who work in large organizations are familiar with the different rhythms associated with different time periods, for example, the accelerated rhythm of sales during the holiday season or the especially fast-paced work of a public agency during "budget season." We also recognize that different places or even different groups have different rhythms. In our interview, the opera singer Elisabeth Catbas related this question to her travels: "I've traveled all over the world. Many different cities have their own rhythms. Some places are much slower and more relaxed. Other places are very hectic. You might enjoy the change or you might find it and be uncomfortable. If you're stuck someplace you have to adapt your rhythm to that place." Of course, the same is true of different organizations.

There is, however, another way in which we use the term rhythm, and that is to denote a certain consistency, pattern, or flow of movement. For example, we might comment on the rhythm of Annika Sorenstam's golf swing, or note, on admittedly rare occasions, when she seems "out of rhythm." We might also remark, as baseball commentators often do, on the fact that on a given evening a pitcher and catcher seem to be in good rhythm, that is, they are on the same "wave length." And isn't it interesting that the term "wave length" refers in science to a measurement of periodicity or rhythm? In the same way, we can often sense when a leader seems out of synch with a particular group.

Finally, we can use the term *rhythm* to describe the "feeling tone" of a song, a dance composition, or even an organization. When we earlier described the difference between a slow and a fast tempo, we very naturally used terms that actually described the feeling evoked by the rhythm, as opposed to the change that one might make in a metronome to accommodate a different pace; we described *adagio* as being "lyrical" and *allegro* as being "spirited." But, interestingly, the connection between tempo and feeling tone works in both directions. On the one hand, your psychological state affects your personal rhythm as you move through the day and also affects your perception of time, as we acknowledge with the comment, "Time flies when you're having fun." On the other hand, the pace, the tempo, the feeling tone of things around us can speed up, slow down, or otherwise complicate our personal and group rhythms. That is simply to say that rhythm can affect our moods and the moods of those around us.

What is most important for rhythm and leadership is the relationship between rhythm and emotion or feeling. Earlier we pointed out that our understanding of time is shaped by our personal experiences and perspectives. While we ordinarily think of time in a linear, mechanical sense, time is really subjective in nature, tied to the personal and culture orientations of individuals and groups. Time is experienced in terms of the occurrence of particular events, and those with substantial emotional content in particular are rarely connected directly to clock time. For that reason, time is capable of infinite variation and indeed varies across groups and across cultures.

Nowhere is the interaction of time and experience clearer than with respect to rhythm. We talked earlier about the difference between allegro and adagio. Typically in dance, allegro segments are shorter, simply because the dancers get tired. But if you ask members of an audience which took longer in clock time, they will likely say that the allegro segment did. This is because they relate to their personal experience of the energy expended by the dancers. We understand that Mikhail Baryshnikov almost never performed a segment over a minute long, but the audience thought he was up there for hours. Dance educator John Wilson of the University of Arizona commented, "Rhythm is not that clock on the wall. Rhythm is always an experienced phenomenon." In the same way, a period of allegro rhythm in an organization may be brief, but it may be experienced as more intense and longer by participants.

When we talk about rhythm, therefore, we are not merely talking about the ordering of time into discrete and recurring structures. Rather, we are talking about how our experience of life itself is revealed. Rhythm is not just a matter of counting the beats or hearing how quickly they pass. To say that something is more rhythmical than something else is not to say that it's louder or more insistent, but that it has "a more compelling or captivating" quality. It is a matter of the quality of the emotional understanding, not a matter of quantity or volume. Rhythm, then, extends throughout the human experience, connecting the vital aspects of that experience in meaningful and recognizable ways. Rhythm organizes our experiences not merely in terms of cadence, but as a way of ordering the emotional content or the feeling tone of a pattern of activities.

For this reason alone, time, and especially rhythm, is essential to effective leadership. If leadership involves touching the emotions and if rhythm guides and orders the emotions, then an essential element of leadership is understanding, responding to, and perhaps even shaping rhythmic experience. But there's another point that makes this issue even more important. Time and rhythm are concerned with movement from the past through the present and into the future. Leadership may draw on the past, and leadership occurs in the present, but leadership is concerned with the future, with the path or direction people take, with the window of time they select to bind their movement. Leadership has to do with helping individuals and groups to understand time more completely, to know their role in the unfolding of events, and to organize their moments to attain a future they desire. Time in this sense, not time as minutes, hours, and days, not time as money, but time as the unfolding of human experience, is the currency of leadership.

The Roots of Rhythm in the Human Experience

One of our students, Janet Woolum, is a superb bowler, a former member of the U.S. national team and a gold medalist at the 1995 U.S. Olympic Festival. In bowling, amateurs can compete in professional tournaments without giving up their amateur status, so Janet thought she would enter a professional tournament. Naturally, she was trying to be attentive to the etiquette of bowling, which includes waiting until the bowlers on the lane on either side of you have started their approaches before you step onto the lanes for your turn (that's called "lane clearance"). In a tournament, you get into a pattern of when it's your turn based on this lane clearance factor. But after a while Janet noticed that some of the pros, including a woman whom she had idolized as she was first learning the game, were giving her questioning or even nasty looks. She had no idea why.

At a break, a friend pointed out what was going on. She said, "Watch those people who are bowling now and you'll see a particular rhythm to who follows who at what time. Without even talking about it, these bowlers have established a certain rhythm that they follow and expect others to follow in a tournament." Janet quickly realized that, in this tournament, the "clearance" was six lanes on either side, but she had been waiting only for three lanes to clear, which meant that she was way out of the rhythm. Without in any way intending to do so, Janet had broken the rhythm these bowlers were accustomed to and it was throwing off their game. That's why they were upset. But once she had recognized the rhythm, she was able to adapt to it herself and everything went much more smoothly.

Most of us are not trained to think about, encouraged to talk about, or called upon to sense rhythms as well as we could. As a result, many of us simply no longer notice how deeply rhythm is rooted in the human experience. Gaining a clearer sense of rhythm and the role it plays begins with becoming more aware of it and consciously paying attention to its effects. Though we rarely think of it this explicitly, rhythm permeates all that we do. As Havelock Ellis, an early writer on dance, put it: "The joyous beat of the feet of children, the cosmic play of the philosopher's thought rise and fall according to the same laws of rhythm." Think of the roots of rhythm, as they exist in our basic physical makeup. The body has a variety of built-in sources of rhythm, starting with the beat of our hearts and the regularity of our breathing. Next is the pendulum-like movement of our limbs, especially our legs, which, when we walk, display a certain rhythm that clearly distinguishes one person from another. (As an experiment, the next time you are waiting for a plane, try imitating, just in your mind, the various rhythms of people walking through the airport.)

These very essential rhythmic functions of the body are related in obvious ways to the emotions. Fear can increase the rate of our heartbeat or accelerate our breathing. Conversely, a sudden "skip" of a heartbeat immediately draws our attention and raises concerns about what that might mean. Similarly, a strong attraction to a person or object can increase the speed of our walking in that direction, while a sense of calm and "taking it all in" will slow our pace.

Rhythmic patterns and variations are also a part of our natural environment. Most obvious are the passing of days and nights, the procession of the seasons, and the movement of celestial bodies through the heavens. Somewhat more subtle, though not completely unrelated, is the rhythm of rain falling on a tin roof, that of a galloping horse or that of ocean waves crashing against a rocky coast. There is even rhythm in visual patterns, such as the spacing of trees growing in a forest or the undulation of a curved line in a painting, a design, or a seashell. And there is the often irregular flow of events through time, classically illustrated by a cat running across the floor, leaping onto a table then off again, continuing its run on the other side.

Rhythm is a part of us and rhythm is all around us. For this reason, it's not surprising that as human beings we share certain rhythmic patterns that enable us to engage one another more effectively. Indeed, rhythm can be seen as the very basis for human interaction. Some have even traced these tendencies back to the rhythmic rocking and patting of infants by their parents. These actions are common to all civilizations throughout recorded history, and reinforce our natural tendencies toward "mutuality" or belonging, saying to the infant that "everything is okay, we're here with you."

These basic and essential human sensitivities become elaborated as we move through life and provide an important basis for interacting with others and finding meaning in that interaction. They become means for "arousing interest, riveting joint attention, synchronizing bodily rhythms and activities, conveying messages with conviction and memorability, and ultimately indoctrinating and reinforcing right attitudes and behavior." In other words, it is the rhythm of mutual emotional engagement, as when we dance together or march together or work together, that brings back something of that state of undifferentiated consciousness we left behind as infants. It may even elicit "echoes of the fetal condition when a major . . . stimulus . . . was the mother's heartbeat."

As we grow, we experience a wide range of movements and sensations that involve increasingly more complicated human rhythms. From very basic actions such as standing, turning, reaching, pushing, pulling, lifting, pressing, striking, or throwing, we learn to sense the difference between an awkward movement and a coordinated movement, the latter always being more efficient and more pleasurable. At least on a physical level, we learn how the various components of any action pattern "fit together," how the elements contribute to the whole.

Consider all that's involved in just throwing a ball, something we think of as a fairly mundane activity. You grasp the ball, you lift the arm and bend it in a certain direction, you move the arm forward at a particular speed, triggering a sequence of "firing" first the shoulder muscles, then the elbow, then the wrist, until you release the ball from your fingers at exactly the right instant. There's really quite a lot involved. But even more fascinating is the way in which it all comes together. Things have to happen at just the right time and in just the right sequence for the ball to travel even a short distance.

Imagine the discipline and coordination that is involved when a major league pitcher like Randy Johnson throws a baseball. The six-foot-ten-inch Johnson throws a fastball that travels nearly a hundred miles an hour and (typically) crosses the plate with incredible accuracy. By snapping his wrist slightly at the point of release Johnson can throw a "slider," a pitch that curves in toward a right-handed batter. Again, the key point is how the various elements of the pitch come together, how each follows its predecessor at just the right moment and with just the right tempo. What is perhaps most remarkable when you consider Randy Johnson's pitching is not just the sheer power that he generates (through a remarkably efficient pitching motion), but the smoothness of his delivery, his coordination. Everything seems to flow so evenly. The pitch is not effortless by any means, but when you compare Johnson's pitching with that of others, the ease and efficiency—that is, the rhythm—of his pitching is striking (pun intended).

Rhythm, then, involves energy in motion. It involves action and rest, control and release, tempo and duration. But the ultimate function of rhythm is to hold patterns together. Whether we are talking about the simplest movements of a child or the more skilled and complex movements of a professional athlete or dancer, rhythm refers to the way in which the various elements are organized into an increasingly coherent and efficient whole. We experience as rhythmical those actions in which the various phases of the movement seem to be well organized or coordinated. They flow together. So we might say that a figure skater moved with special grace and rhythm. Or we might comment on how smooth and elegant the prima ballerina was during the dance performance, how rhythmical she was. Or we might talk about the rhythm Randy Johnson displayed on May 18, 2004, when he pitched a "perfect game" for the Arizona Diamondbacks.

The smooth and measured release of energy, then, is the basis of human rhythm whether on the ball field, in the boardroom, or at the ballet. In this sense, we can even talk about rhythm outside the world of movement and in the world of the visual, the auditory, or the tactile. We might comment on the rhythm of a painting by Degas, a classic show tune such as "Oklahoma," or even that of the line of a beautiful piece of jewelry. There is even a rhythm to other forms of human activity such as thinking or feeling. Margaret H'Doubler, whose work on rhythm in dance and elsewhere is remarkable, put it this way: "The rhythms of song and poetry and the cadences of speech are as much manifestations of organic rhythm as breathing, the heart beat, walking, running, or any other muscular action. Expressive acts are necessarily rhythmical." In all these cases, we experience rhythm as a unifying force, a flow of energy, well constructed, well coordinated, and, ultimately, highly pleasurable to those who engage it.

As we already noted, while the rhythmic release of energy is a constant element of human life, it is a force we rarely are even aware of. We typically don't notice our breathing, the beating of our heart, the swinging of our arms when we walk, or the measured clip of our gate itself. Only in two cases do we normally become aware of our rhythms: one, as we noted before, when there is some disruption in our normal rhythmic pattern, such as our tripping over a rock as we walk, or two, when we either experience ourselves or see in another an unusually well-integrated or coordinated display of rhythmic expression. Rhythm is so much a part of our lives that we simply don't recognize it. That point is of special relevance to our interest in leadership, because it makes it easier for us to understand that in the interactions of human beings, and even in group and organizational life, there may be rhythmic structures that we don't even recognize from day to day, but that may be of profound importance.

So far we have spoken of those rhythms that are a part of a single individual's makeup. But now consider how an individual's rhythms are influenced by the world outside, either the physical world or the social world. Most obvious are the rhythms of night and day and the patterns of human activity that correspond to those—what we know as "circadian rhythms." Under natural conditions, both plants and animals adapt to the day/night cycle of the earth's rotation even though studies have shown that "natural" rhythms may be slightly different for some. But we adapt. We are "entrained" to the twenty-four-hour rhythm so that, for example, we normally sleep at night and work in the day. Again, these rhythms become so much a part of us that they go without notice until we happen to alter the pattern, for example, as we move from one time zone to another and experience "jet lag," or as we take on unusual work assignments such as the "graveyard" shift. The physiological adaptations involved in making these changes are easier for some people than for others, but they can be biologically and behaviorally costly and are rarely complete.

What is most important for our purposes is the way that people adapt their rhythms to those around them in social situations. We change our rhythms in response to the acts of other people just as we change in response to shifts in the physical world. Every facet of human behavior is characterized, organized, and even controlled by rhythmic processes, many of which we are almost totally unaware of. And having a sense of that rhythm is important, because rhythm is the pulse of what we do and feel. "In relation to organization, rhythm may be considered as the process by which events taking place in time are marked off, related, and organized. Without it, all would be confusion."

How Rhythms Interact with One Another

We told the story earlier of Anne Petron and Claude LeClair, two executives who work in an international financial management firm. Specifically, we described the vastly different energy levels they appear to bring to their work. But we might have also said that they bring different rhythms to what they do: Anne appears to work at a much faster pace than Claude—though again we must say that both are highly effective in what they do. But what happens when they have to work together, which they often do? To be honest, initially they struggled. Anne found Claude far too slow and measured, and Claude found Anne a little bit "frantic."

Claude and Anne talked openly about their differences and decided to seek the advice of a consultant/counselor/coach whom they both trusted. Dr. Susan Choe, a psychologist, had a simple but elegant solution. Where she had previously met with each of the two executives in their own offices, for their joint session she selected a "neutral" site, a small alcove in the executive dining room. She asked Anne and Claude to sit across the table from one another and take a few minutes to relax and put aside the work they had been involved in that day. Then she asked that they start a conversation about something completely separate from their work—the weather, the new and very well-reviewed restaurant downtown, the local football team, skiing in the mountains, whatever. After just a few minutes of conversation, she asked each to describe what was happening to them in terms of the rhythm of the conversation. The answer was obvious. They were beginning to "pace" each other in terms of rhythm. They had found a common rhythm that enabled them to communicate more effectively. To this day, when Anne and Claude need to speak at length, they almost always find a "neutral" spot, take a few minutes to get "in rhythm," then begin their work.

What Anne and Claude experienced is not at all unusual. Our own personal rhythms interact with those of others, and vice versa. Indeed, studies have shown that individuals seem to exchange "signals" that can actually affect one another's physiologies, including sleep rhythms, surges of positive feelings, and even immune functions. Laboratory studies have shown that two people involved in a good conversation begin to mirror one another's rhythms, even with respect to physiological factors such as heart rate. "As the conversation begins, their bodies each operate at different rhythms. But at the end of a simple fifteen-minute conversation, their physiological profiles look remarkably similar—a phenomenon called *mirroring*."

The same phenomenon holds true in families, groups of friends, sports teams, work groups, and among professional associates. Mirroring connects and enhances the emotional states of those involved. "Matching or imitating another person's expressed states can evoke similar psychological and bodily states in oneself, thus making it possible to enter into or share the other's feeling." In a group, a team, or an organization, we recognize when everyone is on the same "wave length." Each of us apparently affects the rhythm of others and is affected by their rhythms.

Some people, however, seem to have special impact in ordering the flow and energy involved in human activity. Anthropologist Edward Hall, whose pioneering work on time and rhythm we mentioned earlier, comments on this point as he tells the remarkable story of a study conducted by one of his students. The student decided to see what he could learn about the rhythmic behavior of children on a playground. He filmed the children during recess, and then studied the film of their activities in great detail.

After watching the film several times at different speeds, he noticed one very active little girl who moved from group to group, seemingly attuning each to her rhythm. According to Hall, "He realized that this girl, with her skipping and dancing and twirling, was actually orchestrating movements for the entire playground!" Moreover, when the student took the film to a friend to watch, the friend immediately recognized the rhythm as familiar. He pulled a recording off the shelf and synchronized it with the film. Once this had been done, the music and the film of the playground stayed in sync for a full three-and-a-half minutes. Remember: the music came later. The children did not hear the music while they were playing; their rhythm just happened to match that of the recording.

There are three lessons here that are relevant to leadership. First, as we noted above, the film shows that groups of many kinds operate according to rhythmical patterns. If we can find rhythmic expressions on a playground, we would certainly expect to find them elsewhere, in other groups and organizations. Second, within a particular culture, the same rhythmic pattern that moves people in one situation can be found in others as well. Both the children on the playground and the band in the recording may have been reflecting a larger cultural rhythm familiar to both. Third, the girl who seemed to be "orchestrating" the rhythm of the playground demonstrates the effect that one person can have on the rhythm of a group. We certainly recognize the negative effect of that influence in the expression, "One bad apple can spoil the barrel," which we might interpret by saying that one group member whose behavior is destructive to the rhythm of the group can wreak havoc in the group's process. But we might also suggest the opposite: that one person can also exert a highly positive influence on the patterning of energy or the rhythm of a group. That person we would probably call a leader.

Different societies or cultures operate with differing time perspectives and with different rhythms. But the same is true of groups and organizations. Various groups, organizations, and societies display different time perspectives, they position themselves differently with respect to their history and their development, and the resulting variations present interesting problems as these groups attempt to reconcile their differences. The reason for this is that, as the great choreographer Doris Humphrey pointed out, "Rhythm is the great organizer. Habits of accent form to hold an organism together, patterns of rhythmical shape lend sense and sensibility to life, and the unrhythmical mass of matter is anarchistic, chaotic, a menace to all organization." Similarly, social scientists have argued that rhythm helps "to bind human beings together into emotionally vibrant groups that give meaning and purpose to human experience." Rhythm is at the heart of human interaction; indeed, rhythm is the *heartbeat* of human interaction.

The Tempo of Groups and Organizations

Consider the story of a genetic engineering company that brought together a number of scientists from the world of molecular biology and a number of finance-based, entrepreneurial managers to form the company. The scientists, mostly drawn from academic backgrounds, saw their work as having an internal logic in which problems were seen as evolving from the work itself, making the process of setting specific, fixed targets quite difficult. The executives, on the other hand, were being buffeted by external demands for immediate results and found the scientists' plans not only ambiguous but also unrealistic in terms of the demands of business.

As you might expect, the scientists, accustomed to working at a careful pace and oriented toward long-term contributions, experienced continual pressure from the executives to focus and to accelerate their work so as to provide short-term gains. In their characterizations of one another, the realist managers felt like they were constantly having to contend with immature dreamers, while the scientists felt they had to protect their work, which they saw as the lifeblood of the company, from the myopic managers. The conflicts that resulted almost destroyed the company.

For leaders, the way in which shifts in the rhythms of groups and organizations come about is of special importance. Rhythms are associated with varying degrees of force (intensity, accent, stress) and consume time in their passing (duration), all elements that the potential leader must recognize and employ in his or her work. As H'Doubler wrote many years ago, "An appreciation of rhythm in its simplest beginnings can contribute to the [individual's] realization that rhythm is the universal and controlling force back of all phenomena and that the elements of rhythm exist in all things. It can help him to tune in with the varying rhythms and stresses of life about him. Rhythm in this larger meaning is the form through which all life is experienced and expressed."

Different people, groups, organizations, and societies operate at different tempos. We've all encountered people who operate their lives at a faster pace than others. They dash into the office in the morning, scan pages of briefing papers in seconds, literally run from one meeting to the next, stopping along the way only for short conversations, and dash through phone conversations, finally stopping for a hurried lunch before starting all over in the afternoon. Meanwhile, others stroll through the front door just before nine, conduct lengthy and relaxed conversations around the coffee pot, slowly and carefully read through correspondence or reports, spend time freely with others, often asking not only about work but about personal matters as well, then savor a satisfying lunch with friends before returning to the office for a quick nap before taking on the afternoon.

Most of us, of course, are somewhere between these two extremes, but the interesting thing about these characterizations is that while we recognize the personality differences, the differences in rhythm, we can't be sure which individual is the most productive or which might be the better leader. We can be sure, however, that if these two individuals are forced to work closely together they will drive each other crazy. Donna Maytham, one of the founders of the Richmond Ballet, compared herself with a friend in a way that will probably seem familiar to many: "Our sense of timing is off. I'm go, go, go and she's oooooh so slow."

What we have said about the differing rhythms of individuals can also be said about different groups. Again, an illustration from the world of dance is a good beginning point. In our interview, Kent Stowell, artistic director and choreographer of the Pacific Northwest Ballet (PNB), described the way in which a dance company adopts a particular rhythm. "Our company has an internal rhythm when it dances. And it functions best when it's on the clock that we've set in their bodies and their minds. It brings them to where they can function best. And it has to do with how we do the steps, at what time, and the phrasing of them." Francia Russell, also artistic director for the PNB, made an important point about the feeling of being out of one's normal rhythm: "Doing anything different is like being jet-lagged."

While it's easy to see how rhythm would be built into a dance company, rhythm is also built into groups and organizations, though here rhythm is often more subtle. In our interview, William Post, president and CEO of Pinnacle West, one of the country's leading energy companies, commented, "The rhythm of our tax department is completely different from that of our 'troublemen' and completely different from the people who run the coal plant. So there's a different rhythm. Or different subrhythms." A part of the difference has to do with the cultural and emotional patterns that the different units reflect, something that probably has roots in the varied professional backgrounds of those in the different areas, and a part is probably the result of patterns of socialization within the company. Certainly a major expression of the difference is the tempo or pace of work, something largely based on the way those in different areas view time.

Another wonderful example of conflicting rhythms, this from the world of dance, was related to us by dancer and choreographer Celeste Miller, who teaches a dance class at the Liz Lerman Dance Exchange in which the youngest student is a four year old and the oldest is in her seventies. Miller marveled at the interaction:

> As you can imagine, the rhythms of the room are very interesting. So we take a walk around the space to get people acclimated. And it's these tall trees moving through space—and there's all this frantic action—zoom, zoom, zooming through it. I continually try to find ways as a facilitator to acknowledge for the room that I know that's going on and they should know it's going on too. Because we'll get some older people who are completely freaked out by just the physical noise level of the stuff that's happening in the room. So I begin to figure out exercises where the slower movers can take a slower moving stance and have as their partner a fast mover so they are actually together creating something that doesn't exist unless those two energies are brought together.

She continues,

> Then we reflect on what has happened. We pause and ask people, what was your insight? What was your curiosity? What was your discomfort? How did you take your discomfort and how did you solve it? If the young kid says "I want Dorothy to jump up and down with me," and Dorothy says, "I can't jump up and down with you; my knees won't do it," then the next thing I know the two of them have solved it. Because the need was put out there, the real reason Dorothy won't jump up and down is laid out on the table, and the two of them solve together how they can get the dual energy that they need and not destroy Dorothy's knees.

In addition to the rhythmic differences among different divisions within the same organization, there are marked differences among different organizations. Lattie Coor, former president of the University of Vermont and later president of Arizona State University, remarked on the rapid changes that have occurred in the business world over the last twenty years or so, and the resulting need for businesses to accelerate their tempos. But, he noted, similar changes in pace have not occurred in the university world. "Universities have not undergone, as our critics point out, a fundamental change in the rhythms by which they operate." Here the pace of teaching and research has, perhaps for very good reasons, remained more constant. But, according to Coor, the leader of a university has to understand the language of the quick turnaround business world. As a result, Coor saw part of his job as "simultaneous translation," making sure those operating at one rhythm communicate with those moving at another.

Some companies experiencing high-velocity environments, that is, particularly rapid changes in the market and in technology, have been able to adapt the pace of their decision processes and their operations to accommodate their new environments. Others have not. Certainly the corporate leaders we talked with were quite aware of the changing pace of business conditions that Lattie Coor mentioned. Nearly all described the faster pace of business today as one of the most striking changes they had faced in their careers, and they spoke eloquently about how they have tried to cope with the rapidity of decision making today.

A special case in the rhythms of human interaction occurs when a new leader arrives and attempts to establish a new rhythm in the organization. We witnessed such an occurrence recently at a major American university that had operated with great success under the leadership of a distinguished, even revered, president. The rhythm of that individual and, perhaps not coincidentally, the rhythm of the university was one that might be described as careful, balanced, even-handed, stable, uniform, gracious, sensible, gentle, and unhurried, but also creative, positive, and quite effective. The new president brought a dramatically different rhythm to the organization, both in his personal style and in his expectations for the institution. In large part, his agenda seemed to be one of increasing the tempo of work at the university, asking people to do more and more, and to become more active and entrepreneurial in their teaching and research. While few questioned the new president's ideas, all of which made good sense, faculty and especially staff found it extremely difficult to accommodate the new pace the president sought.

This story, we think, is not at all unusual. Over and over, we have heard stories of new executives, even those moving into well-performing organizations, who "hit the ground running"—literally. That is, they were actually running all the time, and they were "driving people up the wall." In one case, someone finally told the new executive: "You've got to slow down so people can get the work done. They are too frazzled and it's your fault." As we will see, sometimes a more even pace is better than a faster pace.

In any case, it's obvious that many new executives, whether in business or in education or elsewhere, are mindful of changes in the environment that suggest the need for a new way of "doing business," a different tempo. The interesting question is how that person can effectively lead the organization in a new direction. There are a variety of answers, some of which we will explore later in this chapter, but the polar positions seem to be either for the executive to try to force a new pace as quickly as possible, even in direct conflict with the existing tempo of the organization, or for the executive to try to match his or her own style to that of the organization, and then try to move it more carefully over a longer period of time.

George Fisher, chairman and former president/CEO of Eastman Kodak, who was previously CEO of Motorola, Inc., cautioned against the first model in this way: "You really have to be careful about throwing too much at an organization all at once. Some people say you can just drive change until everybody drops, but I don't really think that's true. An organization can only take so much and you have to be sensitive to that." On the other hand, some situations seem to demand "emergency" action, even though that action might be risky to the overall health of the organization—and the tenure of the executive.

Just as we would use the word "dissonance" to refer to conflicting sounds, we will use the word "dysrhythmia" to refer to situations in which rhythms are in conflict. "When people or groups with different [temporal] perspective interact, conflicts often arise. Misunderstandings occur when intention and action are judged, by different participants, on different temporal scales. The differences in temporal perspective often go unrecognized by the participants. But the different temporal scales have values associated with them. . . ." Dysrhythmia can lead to substantial disagreement, but participants in the conflict may not even realize what's occurring. In fact, those involved may experience disagreements as being substantive, when in fact they are merely rhythmic in nature. Ultimately, however, individuals or groups experiencing dysrhythmia must ultimately resolve their differences in order for a more unified rhythm to take over and for the group or organization to work with greater fluidity, ease, and efficiency. Even though rhythm passes quietly and we don't often think about it, as we will see, a person attuned to the rhythmic flow of the particular situation will have an advantage in energizing others and will be a more effective leader.

Cycles, Stillness, and Nonmetric Rhythm

When we talk with groups about the art of leadership, the idea of rhythmic cycles is one that always "connects." One workshop participant, Judy Woodruff, talked about the cycles in the state budget office where she works. During budget "season," there is a special intensity to the work as budget proposals come forward from agencies, are examined by budget analysts, and then are negotiated with the budget office, the governor, and the legislature, often with significant input from various lobbyists and support groups. For most participants, the stakes are pretty high. Programs that are extremely important to them are "on the line." Most feel that success in budget negotiations goes a long way toward success during the remainder of the year.

"What is interesting to me, however," Judy said, "is the transition from the work we do during the rest of the year and what we do in the budget season. The other work is extremely important, and we work very hard. But compared to the budget season it sometimes seems like we're standing still." Judy hesitated and seemed puzzled for a moment, reflecting on what she had just said. "It's really curious," she said, pointing out again that the actual work that people did during the budget season probably wasn't much more than they did the rest of the year. "But the way it feels is sure different. It's a different tone, a different feeling, a different intensity."

Cycles

We are all familiar with the cycles that groups and organizations follow, especially those that follow the calendar: workdays and weekends, the holiday rush in a retail firm, the budget cycle in a public agency, or the passing of semesters in an educational institution. "Cycles may repeat themselves at regular intervals or frequencies such as those associated with the fiscal year, or irregularly such as is the case with technology cycles. Cycles may repeat themselves with the same magnitude or with different magnitudes." A regular cycle might be a set of four quarters constituting a fiscal year. But the intensity of the cycles might vary. For example, the first three quarters of a fiscal year might follow a similar pattern of activity and associated stress, but the fourth quarter might show even greater activity and stress, especially as the end of the fiscal year brings about the reporting of performance data, closing of accounts, and the writing of annual reports.

One problem facing organizations is that of making sure there is a reasonable integration of cycles. On the one hand, this can be a problem internal to an organization, as it seeks to mesh its various cyclical operations. For example, in one hospital it was found that medical services, dietary services, and technical services had each scheduled their own daily and weekly activities without regard to those of other units. Consequently many regularly scheduled events occurred at the same time each day or each week, creating special pressures for the staff and disruptions and distress for the patients. (For example, linens were being changed at the same time food arrived.) The obvious solution was to have the various service providers create a unified calendar built around patient needs. The result was less stress for the staff and better care for patients.

On the other hand, a similar question about cycles arises as organizations attempt to match external cycles that are relevant to their operations. These cycles include such broad environmental concerns as customer demand cycles or those related to technological innovation, but also others that are far more routine and practical. For example, consider the story of the Trenton State Prison in New Jersey, which for decades had its guards begin their shifts at 6:20 A.M., 2:20 P.M., and 10:20 P.M., times many would find quite unusual. They did so for a simple and understandable reason—because the local trolley always stopped near the prison just before those times.

Here, and in situations far more complex and consequential than these, groups and organizations have to synchronize their own cyclical rhythms with those with which they interact. These particular cases involve technical scheduling adjustments that, in the big picture, are relatively easy to accomplish. It's important to note, however, that there are other temporal issues that go far beyond mere scheduling changes, sometimes requiring dramatic shifts in the overall rhythm of group or organization. As such, they imply changes in the emotional dynamics of the workplace, something to which effective leaders must always be attentive.

Think, for example, of the way in which the technological cycle having to do with how quickly and how soon written messages can be answered has been changed by the advent of e-mail. Think of the pervasive consequences that this development has had for the speed with which responses are returned and also the time of day at which responses are given and received. On the one hand, we now expect to get an answer within hours or at least a day or two rather than a week or ten days. We also have drastically altered the pattern of times we receive and respond to inquiries. We used to await the mail delivery once each day. But now messages can arrive—and be sent—at any time. For example, how many e-mail messages have you received recently that were composed in the middle of the night? The changes we have made in response to a new technological cycle, we would submit, have caused a huge change in the rhythms of information transfer in most organizations, with implications not only for how we do our work but, perhaps more subtly, how we feel about our work.

Stillness

A second topic, one that grows quite directly from our study of the arts, music, and dance, is the notion of "stillness." While we most often think of rhythm as involving steady pulses or beats, there is a certain way in which rhythm is rooted in stillness. Without stillness, and the spaces it provides between accents or beats, those aspects of rhythm lose their meaning. The marvelous dancer and choreographer David Parsons talked with us about the importance of being perfectly still, so as to provide the most effective contrast to the eventual motion that surrounds the stillness. Similarly, the legendary choreographer Paul Taylor said, "Discovering how to hold still and yet remain active in a way that looks vital is the most difficult of all." Constant streams of energy need the contrast of stillness to have their greatest impact.

No artist with whom we talked made this point more clearly than the extraordinary mime Robert Shields. Shields told us that he started his career at a wax museum, posing for hours as a live model as guests tried to figure out whether he was real or just another wax figure. "I started from stillness, completely centered. From stillness," he said, "you begin to understand the subtleties of motion. From the stillness came this incredible gift, a sense of rhythm rooted in stillness." What is so fascinating about Shields's story is that his rhythm, which is so well perfected in his performance, ties back to stillness. Or to put it a different way, from stillness arises the possibility of achieving a more "organic" rhythm (a point to which we will return momentarily).

The question of stillness is, of course, familiar to those who pursue the creative arts. When we spoke with members of the Miller/Hull Partnership, the American Institute of Architects' architectural firm of the year in 2003, we noticed how they had designed their own offices and workspace in a very open style to facilitate conversation and exchange among all the employees of the firm. It was a buzzing place, even a little noisy. Architect Craig Curtis later pointed out, however, that the creative process benefits not only from lively interaction, but also from periods of quiet reflection. "In order to keep fresh and stay creative, all the architects in the firm have to have quiet time. Some do their creative work on the ferry, others at the kitchen table at five in the morning. But we all respect that and understand." For the creative individual, the artistic process requires a rhythm that balances activity and inactivity, intense motion and pure stillness.

It's interesting to note, as somewhat of an aside, that rhythm and stillness are also at the heart of meditative practices, most of which employ some type of rhythm (breathing, chanting, etc.) to help the person achieve a state of calm and serenity. There seems to be an almost inborn necessity for human beings to balance action and rest, accent and release. The lesson for leaders is almost too obvious: life in the fast lane requires a few rest stops along the way. Only by working occasional breaks into our travel plans will we have enough time and the right kind of time for "refueling," for reflection on where we are going, and for choosing new directions. We talked earlier about the best rhythmic expression involving a sense of wholeness, a sense of balance, and a sense of coordination. Among other elements, that expression requires a balance of activity and stillness.

Nonmetric Rhythm

In thinking through the role of rhythm in the leadership of groups and organizations, a third and related issue that deserves some special attention is what we referred to earlier as "nonmetric" rhythm—not the rhythm of periodic beats and pulses, but the rhythm that expresses the "feeling tone" of the individual, the group, or the organization. In our experience, the most effective leaders not only understand the pace or tempo of a group or organization, even as complex as that can be, but also sense even more deeply the feeling tone that expresses the group's true character. We talked earlier about dancers seeing the world differently, picking up subtle emotional cues that most of the rest of us miss. Leaders also view the world differently; they see more, even in common events, than the rest of us.

Louis Blair, executive secretary of the Truman Scholarship Foundation, described to us a recent visit to the aircraft carrier USS *Harry S Truman*: "You get a palpable sense of rhythm and rocking and rolling on these ships. And not just from the movement. Planes taking off, folks running, lots of motion on deck, but all in harmony, all with a purpose. And you feel it. It's terrific. It's exciting."

Similarly, Robert Johnson, president and CEO of Honeywell Aerospace, spoke eloquently of this capacity in response to our question about sensing the rhythm of an organization. "You can walk in a building. You can walk in a plant. You can walk in a doctor's office. You can get on a highway. It's in front of you. Leading is about using all your senses. It's all there. You can tell when you walk in a factory, the speed at which people are working. You can see if they have their heads up. People tell you where they are and what's cooking without even talking. Fear, excitement, all those things are right there. You can just tell."

There's a lot of talk about the rhythm of an athlete playing "in the zone," a dancer dancing "ecstatically," or a writer "going with the flow." But few people can identify what that feeling is or how to attain it. We would suggest that one key is the individual's capacity to capture the rhythm in a place, a time, or a set of events, and then "tune in" to that rhythm. Perhaps the best illustration of this talent came from a federal executive named Tony Montoya, who responded to our presentation of this idea by saying, "When I am stressing out or struggling ineffectively, it is often because I haven't found the rhythm of the event. When I recognize this, I stop flailing and start observing and feeling my way into the rhythm." Tony suggested that this not only happens at work, but also in his other activities. "For instance, I used to fly fish very regularly. Now, on the rare occasions that I fly fish, I plan on taking a day to find the rhythm of the river. I know when I have found it because you gain a sensory awareness of where the fish are, what they are doing, and when they are about to strike." The knack, the talent, or the gift—pick your word—of capturing the rhythm of a time or place or event is a rare one, but one many leaders would do well to cultivate, both for their own pleasure and for the connection it enables them to make with others, even the fish.

Leading with Rhythm

Many of these ideas seem to come together in the story of Bess Young, the director of a community mental health facility in Tennessee. Perhaps because Bess also sings gospel music in the choir on Sunday mornings, she has a particular sensitivity to the question of rhythm. But that gets ahead of our story. While we were waiting in the reception area of her facility for our appointment, a disheveled and highly disturbed middle-aged man came in screaming profanities and demanding that he be given a new car to drive to Baltimore. "I've got to get to Baltimore," he repeated over and over.

Just as several orderlies began moving forward, Bess herself came out into the reception area from her office, which we later found out she chose just so she could be near the front door. She quietly waved the orderlies away. Her first words to the man were bold and to the point, almost mirroring his own intensity. It was almost as if she had started singing harmony to his lead. But then she took the lead and began to talk him down little by little. She understood, she said, why he had to get to Baltimore and she wanted to help him. But first he needed to get cleaned up and fed. Soon the man accepted her invitation to "stay for a while."

Later we talked with Bess about the rhythms at play in the situation we had witnessed. She told us that her clients have a rhythm to their illness, in the sense that there are certain times of the year that are typically more difficult than others. This time of year, she said, approaching the holidays, is especially hard as people remember faces and places from long ago and want to return. "So we adjust the rhythm of our facility to that rhythm; we're ready for things like this. We also know the moods of our clients, because we have spent so much time out there in the community with them. I knew when that man came in he wasn't dangerous. He just needed some help. What I had to do was find a way to connect with him and bring him in."

Bess then talked about the way in which different employees work at different paces and march "to a different drummer." But she also told us that she felt part of her job was to bring everyone in the facility together, to provide a steady and unifying "beat." That beat, she said, provided the emotional connection that held everyone in the organization together and got them through the difficult times. But we couldn't help thinking about the situation we had witnessed earlier, and so, near the end of our time together, we finally asked, "Why did you have to come out yourself to handle this situation?" "Oh, I'm not sure I did. But I know how my orderlies work. They face some real tough situations from time to time and have their own way of dealing with people. They would have tried to impose our own organization's rhythm on our visitor before he was ready for it. I just provided a little transition time."

A Steady Rhythm

Several parts of Bess's story deserve comment. Clearly, a solid rhythm in a group or organization provides a special grounding both in dance and in leadership. "A steady rhythm seems to establish and sustain a predictable ground or frame against or within which disturbances may arise, comport themselves, and even be ignored." A good rhythm is a sign of a good working order; it lets people know there is something they can count on, something that's regular and predictable. It helps to build a sense of community. But, as we will see in a moment, to say that a solid rhythm is necessary doesn't mean that everyone has to operate in the same rhythm. Nor does it mean that a rhythm should be mechanical, because mechanical is devoid of breath and spirit and energy. But a solid basic rhythm is the starting point. As professor of dance Alcine Wiltz of the University of Maryland told us, "When rhythm is even, it's easy. You can speed up. You can slow down. There's usually a body to support that." But, he continued, when rhythms are uneven, that shows as well.

The process of rhythmic "mirroring" we discussed earlier is applicable here. To begin a conversation with questions such as "How is your family?" or "How was that camping trip last weekend?" not only shows caring and concern, which is essential to effective leadership, but also provides an opportunity for the rhythms of the parties to get "in sync." Conversely, starting a conversation abruptly, especially with a highly paced expression of anger, is bound to create dysrhythmia and make an already difficult conversation even more so. Certainly Bess talked about the need for a steady rhythm, but she clearly demonstrated her capacity to interact with rhythms different from her own.

Commonality

Bess also commented on the need for a common rhythm. Variations in rhythm among groups can sometimes be a positive thing, but there needs to be some commonality. As opera singer Elisabeth Catbas pointed out, singers have their own rhythms, "And if you try to make a fast voice sing very, very slowly, it's not going to sound good. You should get someone else to sing that." The differences in rhythm that different people bring should not necessarily be considered "problems," but opportunities for a wider range of actions. Getting the right person *and* the right rhythm is necessary to effective action. Dance educator Mila Parrish put it this way: "You have to honor and respect that people think differently and they express themselves differently and that may affect the tempo and timing of the group."

Similarly, as we noted earlier, in industry, the rhythm of the information technology division may be different from that of marketing, and that difference may be important, contributing to the overall work of the organization. Indeed, one skill of the successful leader would seem to be the capacity to identify different rhythms, to become adept in different rhythmic structures, and occasionally to translate across rhythmic boundaries. Bill Post of Pinnacle West remarked, "All rhythm is good. It's just being able to identify that and mold the leadership to the rhythm rather than the other way around." On the other hand, there is a need for all members of the group or organization to come together rhythmically at regular intervals.

Dance educator and anthropologist John Wilson gave us a lesson in rhythm to illustrate this point. He described an African tribe that he once studied that came together each year for a particular ceremony and celebration. As the different families and groups started to gather, they danced to different rhythms, some based on as many as seventy-eight beats. But at one point, all would hit the first beat of their rhythm at the same time. That became the starting point for the group's activity, what Wilson called "Beat One." To put it more simply, imagine one person singing or dancing in phrases of four beats and another doing so in phrases of three beats. Even though they are phrasing their work in different ways, every thirteenth beat will still be a common "one," the first beat of a new phrase for all.

Beat One, as applied to leadership, is where groups that differ in their familiar rhythms find common ground. For example, representatives of various corporate divisions come together around a conference table and begin a meeting together with Beat One. Or Beat One initiates a new congressional session after a break in which members of the legislative body returned to the familiar but varied beats of their home districts. Beat One provides a unifying, regular tempo for everyone in the group of organization, a common rhythmic starting place.

Variation in Rhythm

Despite what we have said about the importance of a regular beat, there are at least a couple of reasons why a leader might want to vary the rhythm of an organization. One is to stimulate creativity or new thinking in the organization. When there is a discrepancy or irregularity in rhythm, our interest is stimulated and emotions are triggered. For example, is that sound in the middle of the night a burglar? For the artist, creating alterations in rhythm is often intentional in order to spark an emotional response. In the theater, Professor Roger Bedard told us, a director will often change rhythm or even color to create an effect, looking for "any kind of conceptual images that will cause people to think about it differently. The value of dissonance is to knock us out of our patterns."

Experiencing arrhythmia (an irregularity in the beat) or even dysrhythmia (conflicting rhythms) may open doors to new possibilities, new ways of seeing familiar problems. We mentioned earlier Francia Russell's comment that experiencing new rhythms is like "jet lag" for the dancers in her company. But she also said "It's sometimes good for our dancers to have their rhythms adjusted. It's good for them to be jet-lagged. It should be stimulating for them." It is, of course, precisely the desire to break the normal rhythm of an organization that leads many to send managers to retreats or conferences where they may encounter new ideas or to create "buffer periods"—scheduled time away from the normal "grind" time designed for people to think more broadly and creatively about what they and the organization are doing.

Dancers and leaders also vary the rhythmic pattern of a group or event in order to add interest and excitement; in fact, that's the essence of composition. Certainly choreographers work with such ideas as variety, contrast, climax, transition, balance, clarity, elaboration, sequence, repetition, and harmony in their work, simply because these are elements of composition that appeal to the emotions. The change, the contrast, supports the emotional meaning of the dance. Orderly is not always better than disorderly, repetitious not always better than varied, and insistent not always better than understated. There is, of course, a risk involved in such variations in rhythms, but as choreographer David Parsons told us: "When [variations] don't work, they are very, very painful. When they do work, they keep you excited." For the leader, shaping the rhythm of the organization is a way to appeal to the individual's emotional core, to touch the heart, and to shape the energy that passes among people. It's something that involves a certain risk, but the payoff can be substantial.

Tempo and Pace

Then there's the matter of tempo and pace, something that involves both understanding the rhythm of the group or organization, and offering the possibility of changes in tempo. We asked a number of artists how they see the world, especially how they "pick up" on the rhythms of groups, organizations, or performances. The basic answer was simple: you have to listen. In this sense, listening is not just hearing, but involves all the senses as well as a good dose of intuition. For dancers, a significant part of picking up the rhythm of an individual or a group is kinesthetic; it comes from watching the way people move. But for leaders it's a matter of gathering information in many different ways, then knowing how to use that information in the best way possible. Changes in the rhythm of an organization are dependent on first understanding the existing rhythm.

The notion of being "in touch" with those in the organization, with understanding their rhythmic capabilities and limitations, was mentioned by a number of the leaders we talked with. When we asked George Fisher of Kodak about rhythm, he knew right away what we were talking about: "Rhythm rings true to me immediately. You want to increase the pace, but organizations are really fragile, and unless you understand the pace and rhythm of an organization you would be in jeopardy of destroying the organization in a day." In fact, being able to sense the rhythm of the organization is a prerequisite to effective leadership. "Most good leaders can sense the energy in the organization and the rhythm—if they are in touch with the organization. There are leaders who are not in touch and work hierarchically—my rhythm or else. Mostly, they don't last long."

Similarly, Bob Johnson of Honeywell Aerospace pointed out to us that an increased tempo can't just be the tempo of the leader; it has to be shared throughout the organization. "I think the leader's job is to find the speed to go around the corners right on the edge, right before we go off the cliff, not slower, not faster. The leader must know whether we can go 70 miles an hour or 90 miles an hour and help the organization go just that fast. But we'll all get there faster if we go the same speed. That might mean that sometimes I take enough time to listen so I don't leave the gate without them. It might mean that we change the engine in their car. But you have to get there together."

What is it that an understanding of the basic rhythm of a group or organization provides the prospective leader? Primarily it seems to be the ground against which changes, variations, and accents can be played out. Understanding the dynamics of a group or organization allows the leader to see and begin to connect the dots, or, to use the language we suggested earlier, to identify the available social energy and to connect the various elements of that energy. But, even more important, it allows the leader to bring together the energy of the group and give it direction and movement into the future.

Timing

With this broader understanding of the rhythmic content of group action, we can return to the question of timing in its more narrow sense. How do artists and dancers think about timing, and what advice might their perspectives hold for leaders? Managers and leaders would all subscribe to the dictum, "timing is everything," typically meaning that choosing the correct time to act is critical to the success of any project. In a rational, scientific sense, timing involves such things as plotting "the probable success of a decision or action in achieving its purpose as a function of when it is inserted in an ongoing plot." Presumably, in this view, increasing the amount and type of information one has so as to increase one's "opportunity interval" or "window of opportunity" could enhance one's timing. Beyond the fact that such a "scientific" conclusion merely states the already obvious, it provides little help to the potential leader who wants to understand timing.

For the leader, timing is a much broader concept and has to do with the intuitive "sensing" of the group or organization and especially the rhythm that characterizes its work. The leader has to comprehend the rhythm of the group, to understand the group's needs and its potential, to articulate a direction for the group, and to trigger group action. That's not merely a matter of deciding that this particular instant is the right moment to move; rather, it's something that brings together the full capabilities of the leader and the group to "set a course" so that they fully capture the power of the available winds. In this, understanding the organizing and guiding force of human rhythm is essential.

Contrary to the rational, scientific view of timing, there's not one "optimum" time to do something. There are many times and each has its own emotional effect. For the musician or dancer, simply hitting a beat a little early adds an element of excitement and energy, while hitting the beat a little late is more sensual. It's really a matter of what effect in terms of social energy you are trying to achieve. Timing is about informing your actions with a clear understanding of your own rhythms and those around you, then designing intuitive and creative responses that advance the flow of energy in a group. According to Celeste Miller, "Timing is about emotional arc, visual arc, a sense of how something needs to unfold, when you reveal things, how quickly you reveal things, foreshadowing, what you want to keep as a mystery, and how you understand what the mystery still is. All of those add up to understanding timing."

Timing is much more a personal matter than a scientific one. It's something that you feel inside and something that you express in the world. Your timing involves the unfolding of events and how you shape that unfolding. Alcine Wiltz of the University of Maryland spoke of timing as "trying to find where the currents are and ride that where the momentum is taking you—to the next meeting, to the next relationship. In dance, that's how we get from one shape to the next. There are many different ways to go but it's all about finding the best organization for what you are trying to accomplish in terms of emotion." In some situations, you may find yourself feeling that your personal "timing" is off, in just the same way a comedian might talk about his or her timing being off. It's a feeling of missing the beat, hitting too soon or too late, being out of touch. Where that occurs, the best advice is to pull back and try to find and adjust to the rhythm of the group, then to see how your own personal rhythm connects. Carla Perlo, the executive/artistic director of Dance Place in Washington, D C., told us, "Knowing when to move requires sensing what's around you, the rhythm. Timing must connect with rhythm. When you change rhythm, you can lose your timing—but if you keep going you'll get it back. You need lots of practice to get good at it."

Change

Finally, it's important to realize that the notion of rhythm implies a particular understanding of change, one as applicable to the world of leadership as to the world of art. The philosopher Suzanne Langer has discussed this idea in considerable detail, pointing out that "The essence of rhythm is the alteration of tension building up to a crisis, and ebbing away in the gradual course of relaxation whereby a new build-up of tension is prepared and driven to the next crisis." Rhythm can be steady, but it is ever changing, providing at least the potential for, if not the realization of, emergent patterns. The beats provide the obvious structure, they constitute moments of stability, but, between each accent, there is an open space, an opportunity, begging to be filled. Rhythm is therefore fully exemplary of the tension between stability and change that is the essence of life and of leadership. Every moment of stability also contains a million possibilities. Rhythm is "always a dialectical pattern in which the resolution of tensions sets up new tensions; the recession of one color brings its complementary to the fore, while our close attention to the latter exhausts its domination and lets the former advance again."

The rhythms of groups and organizations also are marked by a tension between realities and possibilities and it is the daunting, but often exhilarating task of the leader to move into the spaces that represent the possible. These are the spaces where the leader gathers and arranges the social energy that will ultimately move the group forward. But throughout, there is the backdrop of tension and release. The wildly creative and inventive choreographer Isadora Duncan put it this way: "All movement on earth is governed by . . . attraction and repulsion, resistance and yielding; it is that which makes the rhythm of dance." Of course, that's also what makes the rhythm of social change. University president Lattie Coor spoke to us about change in exactly these terms: "A large, complex organization like a university has a limited tolerance for major initiatives. And then it needs a resting period, a digestive period. There are in fact a sequence of steps that need to take place as the change is unfolding, as it is being pursued, as it is being done, as it is celebrated, and then rested." Understanding that change occurs "in rhythm" and understanding the rhythm of change can only help the potential leader.

Reprise

Recall our earlier illustration of the cat running across the floor, leaping onto a table then off again, continuing its run on the other side. In many ways, this is a good metaphor for what happens when leadership occurs. A body is energized, moves fluidly through time and space, encounters obstacles, surmounts those obstacles, and continues on the other side. It all occurs in rhythm and in time. Where leadership is at its best, there is a sense of freedom, a sense of flow, even a transcendent character—a moving beyond the moment and confronting the future. We clearly understand today that leadership is not a blow to the head; it's not a matter of power. Leading involves drawing energy forward, organizing that energy, and stimulating its movement through time and space in a rhythmic way—that is, in a smooth and coordinated fashion characterized by ease and efficiency. Getting energy to flow through time and space is not accomplished by force but by tapping into the rhythm of a group or organization, by capturing the spirit embodied in that rhythm, and by allowing the smooth progression of that rhythm into the future.

Some leaders intuitively understand the dynamics of rhythm in the groups and organizations of which they are a part. But others can increase their skill in this area. After all, rhythm is so easily accessible; it's a part of our basic makeup, the way we move and the way we act. But too often we let the rhythms of human interaction pass unnoticed. In contrast, a conscious recognition of patterns of rhythm provides an important basis for leadership. Leaders must know and be able to "play" with the rhythms of their groups and organizations. Only in this way will they be able to shape the energy available to the group so as to allow the group to join the flow of unfolding events with a smooth and even tempo, with rhythmic ease and efficiency, with the coordination of thought and action that is the characteristic of groups that have been energized, that is, groups that have experienced real leadership.

4

Communicating in Images, Symbols, and Metaphors

Two women are standing in the hallway talking together. One rolls her eyes and sighs. Another puts her hands on her hips, looks down, and shakes her head. A third one walks up and said, "I thought we agreed not to talk about our children anymore."

A leader tells us that in order to lead others, first you have to know yourself. "Only when you understand yourself and the particular filters you use to sort out what's going on can you accurately understand what's happening with others."

A senior executive brings her top management team together after a particularly trying time for her personally and for the business. She speaks from the heart, not the head, about what the organization and her managers mean to her. After she finishes, an overwhelming sense of caring and concern fills the room.

A corporate CEO told us, "The science of leadership is to take the simple and make it complicated. The art of leadership is to take the complicated and make it simple."

Over many years, artists develop both skills and insights that enable them to relate to others at a very basic human and emotional level. Watch a gifted dancer or actress perform and you will see how she begins to connect with the audience emotionally, to draw them in, to make them feel a part of her world, and to cause them to feel something special. In part, artists connect by fashioning images, symbols, and metaphors that appeal to an intelligence far different from that of the intellect. They employ a language that carries strong emotional power or ascendancy, a language that speaks to the human spirit. They connect by relating to those primal human experiences or "stories" that we all share: the myth of the hero or the tale of love lost and then redeemed. They resurrect familiar tales and common experiences, and we find ourselves caught up in feelings and emotions we may not have even realized we had.

If you see dancers practice or perform close up, as we have done recently, you will realize how physically demanding dance is. In most dance, there is a great deal of athleticism. Yet dancers are not out there on the stage to set records for the highest elevation or the fastest pirouettes. Dance is not just about choreography, doing the steps, and certainly not about records. Rather, as Andre Lewis, artistic director of the Royal Winnipeg Ballet, told us, "It's about dancers making that connection, through their movements, through their personality, even through their occasional lack of movement."

In fact, when new dancers are auditioning for a ballet company, assessing their ability to connect is extraordinarily important. When we asked Roy Kaiser, artistic director of the Pennsylvania Ballet, what he looks for in the best dancers, he responded: "I look for dancers that have the physical capabilities to perform classical ballet. You need a body with good proportions, certain attributes, extensions of the hips, things like that. But the special dancers have something that comes from within that changes dance from a series of steps to movement. Pure joy or sorrow—either one—can come out of the same group of steps." Dance is about the communication of emotional experiences that cannot be explained or reduced to a matter of fact.

Interestingly, many of the leaders we talked with were equally insistent that their work, the work of leadership, is all about "making connections." Indeed, many seemed to describe that ability to connect as the essence of leadership. Jeanette Harrison, director of Knowledge and Learning at Intel, put it this way: "You have to feed that individual with whatever psychic energy they need to keep going and to do even greater things, not encumbered by the past but sometimes taking enormous risks personally and professionally. And it takes connecting with people. You can't be a true leader without connecting." In a similar way, Bill Post of Pinnacle West spoke of the leader's not succumbing to the temptation to "educate" or "train" those in the organization. "If I set out to educate my organization on whatever subject is, I've taken on the wrong task. To educate is not the role. To emotionally connect is. If I can get you to a point where you'll educate yourself on the subject, I don't need to educate. But I do need to emotionally connect. When you start thinking about it, leveraging the organization, it's all emotional." You have to capture the hearts and souls and minds of people. Then you can get their energy.

Again, a comparison between managers and leaders is appropriate. Managers can and do use rational, technical language in their communications; leaders may use such language as well, but they must also move beyond that language so as to connect with people at an emotional level. The difference between acting as a manager and acting as a leader in large part involves changing the way one communicates. Actually, that's something that's fairly easy to observe (though not necessarily easy to do). If you ask a group of managers to describe important projects that they are working on, most will do so in highly objective, rational, and technical language. They will talk about their goals for the project, the resources they have available, the time constraints, and the problems they are encountering. Most will use fairly constrained gestures and maintain a very even tone and temperament.

If you then ask the group to talk about those same projects as if they were leading the project and trying to enlist the help of others, their language, their movements, and their entire demeanor, will change. They will talk with greater energy and enthusiasm, they will convey more feeling and emotion, and they will even use less technical, more image-based language. Again, a part of what leaders communicate is clearly rational and sometimes must be fairly technical. But the part of their communication that makes them leaders and makes the rest of us want to follow is that which connects with us emotionally.

What is the language or currency of that emotional connection? For artists, the answer is easy: their communication occurs less through the use of ordinary words than through images, symbols, and metaphors. Certainly the message expressed in painting or in music is conveyed through imagery rather than words. But the same is true of other arts, and dance is no exception. Philosopher Joan Cass puts it quite simply in saying that "a dance is made up of experiences transformed into images." The language of art is not the language of the technical, mechanical world. It is a language of patterns and abstractions, communicating meaningful characterizations.

Art is about expressions of the human spirit, and such expressions are better communicated in images, symbols, and metaphors. This was stated most eloquently over a century ago by the French writer Stephane Mallarmé in an oft-quoted essay on ballet: "I mean that the ballerina is not a girl dancing . . . but rather a metaphor which symbolizes some elemental aspect of earthly form: sword, cup, flower, etc., and that she does not dance but rather, with miraculous lunges and abbreviations, writing with her body, she suggests things which the written word could express only in several paragraphs of dialogue or descriptive prose. Her poem is written without the writer's tools." As we will see, the leader also writes "without the writer's tools," and often does so in powerful imagery and creative abstraction.

The language of leadership, like the language of art, is especially characterized by the use of images, symbols, and metaphors. The leader's capacity to connect with people emotionally is expressed in many different ways, but here we examine three. First, leaders tend to be more adept than others at a form of hearing and understanding that we will call "empathetic listening," listening for and comprehending the subtle nuances of sound and movement that reflect a person's inner state. Second, leaders more frequently engage in what we term "evocative speaking," skillfully using image-based words and metaphors that evoke a sensory or emotional response in listeners. And, third, there is the matter of physicality and movement. Even beyond the study of "gestures" and "body language," we communicate important physical messages to others and many of those messages are directly relevant to the act of leading.

Empathy and Emotion

One of the best stories of empathetic listening we heard came from Larry Newman, inventor of the ultra-light airplane and a record setting balloonist, who joined Ben Abruzzo and Maxie Anderson for the first successful Atlantic Ocean crossing in a helium balloon. Newman recounted the contest for leadership that took place in front of him during the flight and his own careful observation of what was happening, something that he described as almost requiring "emotional peripheral vision."

In Newman's own words: "I'm really fortunate to see things and notice things that other people don't. So in that gondola I saw everything. Both Ben and Maxie had tried the flight a year before and landed in the ocean in horrific conditions. Ben suffered severe frostbite. On this flight, because it was cold, his foot was bothering him. So we were at a point where we had to throw some stuff away or we were going to land in the ocean. So Maxie said, 'let's throw that heater away,' ignoring Ben's comments about how his foot was really bothering him. And I said, 'Yeah, but Ben needs that for his foot. So let's vote.' We kept the heater." While Larry's listening was empathetic, Maxie's was not—and empathy carried the day.

There is no question that artists, musicians, and dancers are concerned with engaging the emotions. They are concerned with grasping and expressing the inner experience of human life, and empathy and intuition are central to their work. Psychologist Rudolf Arnheim describes the work of artists in exactly this way: "To be sure, artists—whether they are poets, painters, or musicians—have a particularly acute sensitivity in observing the behavior of what surrounds them. They experience this behavior as an interplay of forces . . . images reflecting the inner forces of the human mind—the strivings, the attractions and repulsions that are the central concern of our existence." The artist's empathy and intuition enable him or her to pick up clues to the core of the human experience, something that enables artists to evoke very basic emotions. Importantly, these clues that are gathered are typically expressed in terms of images or symbols rather than words or data.

The same is certainly true of dance. In fact, philosopher Walter Sorrell puts empathy at the center of the creative experience of dance: "It does not matter what the dance is about as long as it creates a high form of empathy." Both the choreographer, acting through the process of designing the dance, and the dancer, through the process of interpretation, must engage the audience in an emotionally vivid sense. The connection that artists make is, of course, not simply intellectual. Rather it is visceral. The artist strives to connect with the viewer, the listener, the audience in such a way that something happens that is personal, emotional, natural, spontaneous, unthinking. Without a sense of empathy for the potential audience, the result will simply be meaningless.

The leader engages his or her "audience" in a similar fashion. The leader must understand potential followers in an empathetic and intuitive way, something we are coming to acknowledge more directly than in the past. We are now coming to recognize the legitimacy of multiple types of human intelligence and that the world of the rational or the intellectual is just the tip of the iceberg, and an extremely deceptive tip at that. What we are increasingly discovering is that human emotions and qualities such as empathy and intuition play a significant role in human life generally, and an especially significant role in leadership.

While this view is gaining increasing acceptance, it was actually somewhat radical just over twenty years ago, when educational psychologist Howard Gardner published his book *Frames of Mind*. Gardner argued that our society tends to evaluate the intelligence of our children in terms of one (and only one) type of intelligence, the kind of intelligence tested by the standard "Intelligence Quotient," or IQ, test. IQ tests presumed that by measuring the child's verbal and mathematical ability, we could determine whether the child was "smart" or not, and that smarter children would be more successful than their counterparts. In contrast, Gardner argued that while these children might have greater academic success, their IQs and their academic achievements do not necessarily translate into more general life successes. Think, for example, of how many people you know with high IQs who are socially inept or who totally lack any artistic talent. And how many people do you know who work for others with lower IQs?

As an alternative, Gardner suggested that there are "multiple intelligences," that is, a wide range or "spectrum" of intelligences, many of which might lead to life success, though in different fields of endeavor. More recently, Daniel Goleman, journalist and behavioral scientist, has offered the phrase "emotional intelligence" to refer to "the sense in which there is intelligence *in* the emotions and the sense in which intelligence can be brought *to* emotions." The idea is that personal or emotional intelligence, understanding oneself and others and acting wisely in social situations based on clarity with respect to one's own emotions, has a great deal to do with the ability to lead a successful life.

In the book *Primal Leadership*, Goleman and his colleagues Richard Boyatzis and Annie McKee have applied the notion of emotional intelligence to the study of leadership, arguing that "Great leadership works through the emotions." That is, a leader needs to be fully attuned to the emotional as well as intellectual impact of what he or she is saying and doing. People will react to the emotional "signals" the leader gives off, and where those signals "connect," individuals *resonate* with the leader. As opposed to *dissonance*, which is created when there is a lack of harmony between potential leaders and followers, the successful leader stimulates *resonance* among those who follow. The leader and the followers are on the same "wave length," they are "in sync," and there is less "noise" in the system. People get along better and work together more effectively. Most of all, the leader's skill in understanding his or her own values and emotions as well as those of others leaves people feeling encouraged, excited, and uplifted, even in difficult times.

Basic to creating resonance is "empathetic listening," which we define as listening for and understanding the subtle nuances of sound and movement that reflect a person's inner state. Empathetic listening is actually not unfamiliar to most of us, though it probably is not as frequently practiced as it might be. Sometimes we recognize that what someone is saying or even showing through their body language is not what they are really feeling. We may even know better what people are feeling than they do themselves. How that happens is inexplicable—at least in rational terms—yet we know that it happens. We suggest that such empathy is at the heart of the leader's craft.

This capacity for empathy is at the base of the capacity for both artists and leaders to "connect" with others at a deep and meaningful level. Carole Couture, vice-president of CommerceHub and former president of ArtSelect International, told us about how important it is for the leader to be able to "know" other people—

not just listen to others, not just hear others, but to know them: "It's about the whole person. You need to get a gauge on who they are. What really drives them. Typically the manager says it's money and the employee says it's being in the know. Let me know what's going on. Let me be part of the puzzle." And we thought Couture was right on target, empathetically speaking, when she added, "It's important to see if they are laughing."

We suggested earlier that the first role of the contemporary and future leader was to help the group or organization or society understand its needs and its potential. Such an empathetic understanding of an individual, a group, or an organization requires very careful listening, both to what is said and what is not being said. It requires building trust and respect in the group, so that people are willing to "open up." It requires creating conditions in which people are willing to come forward and express their good ideas. It requires a sense of insight and discernment, a capacity to sort through the jumble and chaos of another person's mind so as to help them see clearly what was only dimly viewed before. And it requires an intuitive sense of when to ask just the right question, the one that reveals the most.

We talked about this capacity with Hugh Downs, legendary television journalist, who has logged more hours of commercial television that any other individual and who is known for his warm and engaging interview style. Downs noted that others have chosen quite different styles: "There have been people who have enjoyed some success using a 'scalpel' technique. But that usually causes the person you are interviewing to throw up armor. If you relate more and they trust you, you can make them feel more at home and they are likely to reveal more of themselves." And what is it that you are doing while engaged in empathetic listening? Downs responded, "Your cognitive machinery almost steps aside to make room for your emotional and intuitive. So if you sense how someone really feels about something, maybe you don't even think about it, just a look in the eye. An intellectual gets a grip on the world through the rational, but this involves emotions. It may even have its roots in something spiritual."

Other leaders we talked with pointed out that the need for empathetic listening is especially great because the information you need is rarely available in quantitative form. U.S. Air Force general Ronald Fogleman, a former member of the Joint Chiefs of Staff, pointed out that he always had a base of data to work with, but that was only the beginning. "Out of headquarters would come a set of metrics. Everybody ought to know what their abort rate was, their mission capable rate, their cannibalization rate, and all that. That's fine. You could always look at that. But I was more interested in what was behind that. Why did something suddenly start to happen? And normally the answer was not going to be found in the conference room. You'd be out there on the flight line talking with people. You'd be at the bar talking to the pilots. And you'd start sensing that this just isn't right."

The same point was made by George Fisher of Kodak, who was actually trained as a mathematician. "I'm a great believer in quantifying the quantifiable," he told us, "but that's just a starting point. The big leadership decisions are on top of that and come from different feelings, instincts, advice. It sits on a quantitative platform, but it's not quantitative." Once again the line separating leadership from other activities seems to be at the point where you move into the world of emotions, intuition, and feelings.

With respect to the issue of empathetic listening, there are two other questions. First, in what ways is empathetic listening different from the often-prescribed "active listening"? Proponents of active listening suggest that managers have a reason for listening, that they suspend judgment initially, that they resist distraction, and that they rephrase what they are hearing to confirm that they received the right message. Imagine that you come up to someone and ask, "How are you doing?" They respond, "I'm doing well." An appropriate active listening response might be "Oh, you say you're doing well?" But we know there are also situations in which you ask how someone is doing and they respond "I'm doing well," yet you still answer by saying, "What's wrong?" You've heard something or seen something, you've grasped something intuitively that makes you aware that all is not right. That would be an example of empathetic listening.

In any case, the leader needs to be able to enter into the world of another, to be able to hear, to feel, and to understand the meanings, values, and emotions of the other, even when those are only dimly present in the other's own consciousness. In Carl Rogers's somewhat fanciful terms, it is almost like "my inner spirit has reached out and touched the inner spirit of the other." The leader has to listen and to "engage" the other person or the group, meaning both that the leader has to be fully present and engaged in the discussion and that the leader has to extract the most substantial meaning possible.

As a leader, you're not just listening for the words—though that's important. Rather, you are listening and indeed searching for or "mining" the meaning. That requires a very careful and practiced sense of observation. "This means not only looking with a keener eye but listening with a keener ear and responding with keener senses all around, including feeling with greater sensitivity. Then we can begin to see one thing in terms of another and to notice the relationship between one thing and another, growing into a fuller grasp of the value and meaning in symbolism and imagery."

Second, the capacity for empathy is dependent on our clear understanding of ourselves. This is an essential point—that creating human connections is based in substantial part on the leader's knowing him or herself. Actually, acknowledgments of the importance of knowing oneself as a prelude to successful management practice are abundant in the literature in both business and public administration. For the effective manager, self-awareness and related concepts such as self-reflection, self-understanding, and self-control are essential.

While acquiring these capabilities will surely be helpful to leaders as well as managers, the reasons leaders need self-understanding are even deeper and more complex. We see the world through the lens of our individuality and those personal experiences that have shaped who we are. But if we don't recognize that we are seeing the world through a special lens and if we fail to "correct" for the blurring of that lens, we will fail to see the world accurately. While we could quote a variety of psychologists on this point, we thought Thomas Downs, former president and CEO of Amtrak, expressed it quite eloquently when he remarked in our interview: "Self-knowledge is the window through which you see other people and understand the human condition. Most people who are really good at understanding the impact that they are having on another person understand it through their own filter, who they are, what they do, all of the hopes and emotions, all of the aspirations. They understand the human condition. And you can't make that up artificially." If you are to fully live and respond in the most complete way to others, then you must know why your own feelings work as they do. To know others, especially to know others empathically, you must first know yourself.

Evocative Speaking

One of the most interesting stories we heard about the importance of communicating in images, symbols, and metaphors came from Phillip Fulmer, head football coach at the University of Tennessee. Fulmer told us that mid-way through the 1998 season his team was playing well, but he thought that something was needed to keep the team on track: "We were undefeated but we weren't playing our very best football." At about that time, a friend, knowing Fulmer liked to hike, gave him a beautifully carved walking stick. Fulmer was walking to the field when he was presented with the walking stick, so he just continued onto the practice field with his gift in hand. He showed the walking stick to some of the players, and one of them made the comment, "Hey, coach, you look like Moses."

Fulmer's initial reaction was to think of Moses as an old gray-headed bent-over guy—not an appealing image. But later that night Fulmer thought about it again and realized that Moses had led his people to the promised land. He thought, "This might be the corniest thing of all times, but I'm going to do it." In the team meeting the next day, instead of rows, he put the room in circles, so as soon as the players walked in they knew something was up. Fulmer said, "Okay, you guys were being cute yesterday and said I looked like Moses. Well, Moses led his people to the promised land. And I'm telling you right now that we're going to win a national championship and this stick that you were laughing at is going to be the center of our energy, it's going to be the 'synergy stick.' Every time you see this stick, you think of this meeting. When you are on the practice field and sweating and hot and tired and can't go anymore, you see this stick and think of this meeting and that we're going to win the national championship. This is ours. Don't tell your parents, don't tell your girlfriend, don't tell the media. Nobody knows about this but us." From then on, the synergy stick was passed around from group to group at every practice. It was the first thing on the bus, the first thing off. It was the energizing force.

Phil Fulmer understood that leadership is about energizing others and that sometimes that can best be done through the use of imagery and symbolism. That season the University of Tennessee defeated Florida State University in the Fiesta Bowl and won the national championship. Fulmer was named national coach of the year.

In the past, the leader was generally expected to come up with ideas about where the group or organization should go and then move everyone in that direction. Leaders were expected to have a stronger sense of possible future opportunities than others. They were the creative people, at least with respect to the direction in which the group was to move. In part the latitude given to leaders to establish a direction for the organization came from the assumption that from their lofty posts leaders could see things that others couldn't see. In part it was probably also just plain, old-fashioned deference to authority. Goal setting was the leader's prerogative and others shouldn't interfere.

Today we are beginning to modify that view in at least two ways. First, we are increasingly using the term "vision" to describe the direction the group or organization might take. President George H.W. Bush talked about "the vision thing"; businesses and public organizations spend countless hours and days developing vision statements; individuals and families are even encouraged to express their own visions. We suspect that an important reason for this shift in the language we employ is that people have recognized that goals are technical and visions are emotional. Consequently, leaders who want to connect with people at an emotional level consider statements of vision far more powerful—and they are right, at least in those cases where such statements do indeed evoke a shared emotional reality.

Second, our thinking about the leader's role has been changed by the recognition that broad participation in setting the goals, directions, and vision of a group or organization is helpful in arriving at the most comprehensive and creative statement, as well as the one most likely to be implemented. Many groups and organizations are taking more time to work through a broad, participative process of "visioning." Within a small group, that discussion may not be at all formal, perhaps merely an element of the group's conversation, while in a large organization, the process can be extraordinarily detailed and time-consuming. Yet some broad involvement of group members in the process of establishing a vision is increasingly a part of the work of groups and organizations.

Under these circumstances, it sometimes appears that the leader has no significant role. Actually, nothing could be further from the truth. The leader's role remains central to the visioning process. It's just a different role. Instead of coming up with the vision, the leader now must "integrate and articulate the group's vision." In some ways, this is more difficult than the leader's deciding alone. To come up with a vision on your own is certainly a substantial task, but it is even more difficult to guide people through a process where they can examine their beliefs and aspirations in a complete and authentic fashion, to help them sort out the different and complex ideas, desires, and inclinations of the group, then to state the group's vision in a way that resonates with those in the group and helps to establish an identity and direction for the group. We once heard a news analyst respond to a question about whether Microsoft was an innovative company by saying no, that instead Microsoft's talent was bringing together good ideas from many places, making them work together, and triggering those actions necessary to bring those good ideas to the market. In many ways, the leader's talent is parallel. The leader doesn't have to be the one to come up with the good ideas, but the leader must play a substantial role in evaluating what is a good idea and what is not, in reconciling differences, in combining and coordinating viewpoints, in expressing the resulting formulation in a clear and understandable fashion, and in triggering action on the part of the group to move in the desired direction.

This latter activity is, of course, what we identified as the third role of the contemporary and future leader—to act as a trigger or stimulus for group action. To do so requires follow-up and continued effective communications. We think of the vision of an organization as embracing the broadest ideals and aspirations of the group. It is a sketch of "the big picture." But beyond articulating the broad vision of the group or organization, the leader is in fact called upon to help identify and to make understandable the key elements that flow from the vision, the little pieces of the puzzle. The leader is the one who can best express the group's ideals, its identity and its aspirations, and that means communicating with people throughout the organization in a coherent and meaningful way, but also in a way that "connects" with them at both an intellectual and an emotional level. And, as we have already seen, that communication takes places not only at a technical level, but through the use of images, symbols, and metaphors.

Judy Mohraz, president of the Virginia Piper Trust, put it this way in our interview: "One element that's significant in the leadership of many individuals is helping to foster a shared vision. That to me is always *painted in pictures*. It's always something that's articulated in ways that will connect. The more you can paint those images of what may be, then the better able people are to develop the concrete strategies to move in that direction" (emphasis added). The vision of the organization evokes a special recognition and response because it speaks to the heart. And because it speaks to the heart it has the capacity to energize the group or organization—and that is the essence of leadership.

The act of leading involves evoking those feelings and emotions that energize members of a group or organization and in part that occurs because leaders engage in speaking patterns that distinguish their communications from those of others. We call this capacity "evocative speaking," which we define as skillfully using image-based words and metaphors that evoke a sensory or emotional response in those who hear you. In other words, leaders talk differently from others. They have special capacities for communication. They employ language in different ways. They use different kinds of words. They just sound different, and that difference is what enables them to "connect" with others as they do. In this section we will examine several aspects of the leader's capacity for evocative speaking.

The Simple and the Complex

Artists, especially dancers, are concerned with taking things that are complex and communicating them in a clear and meaningful way. Martha Graham, even though she was known for her radical approach to dance, once said, "when a plain walk is right and expresses everything that is to be expressed, more than a walk would be wrong." Many people, accustomed to the elaborate and complex dramatic productions of classical ballet or the intricate and complex movements of modern dance, might be surprised by that statement. They might find it even more surprising that we heard very much the same thing from many of the leaders we interviewed. In one of the most compelling comments we heard, Bill Post of Pinnacle West remarked, "The science of leadership is to take the simple and make it complicated. The art of leadership is to take the complicated and make it simple."

The relationship between simplicity and complexity is itself actually quite complex. In either the case of dance or leadership, making things simple does not mean ignoring the complexity of the topic at hand. It does not mean going back to the beginning, making things naïve, crude, ordinary, or trite. Indeed, it means quite the opposite. It means to make things pure, to seek out the essence of the topic at hand, comprehending all its complexity, yet organizing and expressing it in a way that is clean and precise, comprehensible, unambiguous, coherent, and understandable. A simple statement, in this context, implies a freshness of style and an uncluttered elegance. Most of all, that which is simple goes to the core of the meaning that is to be expressed.

It's really very hard to make things simple. How many people have viewed an exhibition of modern sculpture—for example, the mobiles of Alexander Calder (who, incidentally, designed sets for Martha Graham) or the paintings of Jackson Pollack—and have come away saying, "I could have done that"? But it's not that easy. That which looks simple and straightforward is often the result of an intense creative process in which ideas, impressions, and techniques blend in a most peculiar way to express something in a way that appears simple, but is perhaps better described as "elemental" or "essential," in the sense of going to the essence of something. To engage in such an activity requires a thorough and complete understanding of the entire issue and the intellectual and artistic capacity to bring together the most meaningful patterns of thought and intention, so that the essential can be distilled from the complex. As dance educators Lynne Anne Blom and Tarin Chaplin have written, "Some things are too simple for beginners—trying to get to the essence of something is advanced work."

Again, we may be describing the line between management and leadership. Some managers, and especially some technical people, get tied up in knots when they try to explain things. They make things more complex than we can comprehend. On the other hand, people who really know an issue and can get to the essence of that issue can explain it in ways a child would understand. Albert Einstein said, "Any intelligent fool can make things bigger and more complex. It takes a genius and a lot of courage to move in the opposite direction."

Getting to the essence of any issue requires critical thinking, reflective thinking, and integrative thinking, all coming together as a part of the creative process. Choreographers or the leaders are typically artists who have the capacity to take multiple and even conflicting images and ideas and find patterns and associations that others may not see. They find the unifying themes and impressions, those that express the essence of the matter being communicated. Then they add just enough contrast and variety to make their expression interesting and to connect with the "audience." It's not that they have knowledge or information that others don't; rather, they know what to do with what they have. The key is to employ that material in a unique, expressive, and coherent way—one that connects with others.

For leaders, at whatever level, the capacity to sort through complexity in order to express things simply and understandably is absolutely critical. As a leader, over time you become more educated, informed, skillful, but real leadership comes from taking very complex patterns and bringing about a kind of clarity. It is the ability to interpret reality in ways that really help others understand what may be possible. Whether you are working with a broad statement of vision for the group or organization or working out the details of a new performance plan, the leader will be the one who is able to sort through the complexity, the chaos, and the dead ends, to arrive at a statement that makes good sense and communicates meaning. "When you land on that statement," Carole Couture of CommerceHub pointed out, "it frequently becomes sort of an 'adage' that people repeat, something that makes them remember the goal." (And isn't the word *adage* appropriate here? It refers to a condensed or memorable saying, typically one filled with imagery and metaphorical content.) Couture continued, "It's got to be something that hits home. Once it resonates, people are able to communicate it to the next level and so on." Part of the leader's art, we suggest, is being able to take the complex and distill its essence, then to communicate that message in a meaningful and understandable way, a way that connects with and energizes people.

Closely related to the question of leaders communicating in simple, but meaningful ways is the question of providing people with an appropriate context for thinking about issues facing the group or organization. Leaders offer a message and are well advised to stick to that message, but they also provide followers with a set of lenses with which to view problems that arise. Those lenses may be as broad as the kinds of statements about quality service that often appear in corporate vision statements, or as narrow as a quick comment in a meeting that shifts the conversation in measurable ways. "Maybe we can think about this differently."

Jan Perkins, city manager of Fremont, California, told us that in order to understand the lenses people are using, she pays attention to the questions people ask. "If staff members are dealing with capital improvements, do they just ask the technical questions or do they ask whether members of the community might want something different?" Listening for the questions people ask tells you a great deal about the way they view a situation. Perhaps even more important, those questions reveal the values that people hold. They tell you what they think is important. In a sense, then, setting a context means giving people a way of viewing things and a basic set of questions to ask.

Setting a context also gives people the security of knowing where they stand with respect to what's going on around them. And this can be an especially artistic activity. John Coltrane, the legendary jazz saxophonist, once said, "You got to give your audience something to hang on to." One way to give them something to hang on to is to set the context. Some singer/songwriters, for example, will talk for five minutes about a song before singing a single note. What they are trying to do, of course, is to establish a context for those who will listen. In part, that context is intellectual: this is what the song is about. In part it's emotional: they are trying to establish a certain feeling tone. But you don't have to talk in advance. There is some setting of the context that can occur during the performance itself. Dancer and choreographer Celeste Miller described her efforts with respect to the aesthetics of context: "As an artist I'm interested in whether I have crafted some subtle ways that the audience is actually learning what I need them to learn as a context for the work at the same time that they are experiencing the work itself."

The leader has the same options available—either to set the context in advance or to shape the context as the work is proceeding (or most likely some of both). A perfect example of the first alternative is, of course, the way in which a leader might introduce a topic to open a meeting. Catherine McKee, vice-president of General Dynamics Decision Systems, told us about a staff retreat where she opened with a statement about the meaning of work, that people want to feel called to their work, to find meaning in that work, and not just put one foot in front of the other. "I spoke from my heart and not my head about what those people meant to me. I told them we were custodians of the life experiences and work experiences of those people who look to us for leadership. As a result, the plans we developed were about the people in the organization and about their development. To me, that's more about the artistry of our work and it made a tremendous difference."

The leader can "set the stage" for a discussion, thus substantially affecting the direction that discussion will take. But the leader will also likely continue to develop the context as the "play" progresses. In our interview, University of Oregon president Dave Frohnmayer, who had earlier served as the state's attorney general, recalled, "When I argued cases before the Supreme Court, I thought the role of counsel before those nine august justices was always to keep bringing the argument back to the central flow of the characterization that we wanted the Court to accept. If they agree with your characterization of the problem, you're 85 percent of the way toward getting the Court to buy your solution to the problem." Frohnmayer used the metaphor of a river with many tributaries and saw the leader's role in setting the context as being one of always getting things back to the main flow. Once more, the leader doesn't provide specific answers, but shapes the questions people ask.

In their book *The Art of Framing*, Gail Fairhurst and Robert Sarr explore the way in which managers and leaders shape meaning in their organizations, a skill they call "framing." The idea is that the leader's role is to make sense of things and then put them in terms that are meaningful. A "frame" says which things should be part of the conversation and which things should be left out. Presumably, if the manager can shape the interpretations people bring to their work he or she will substantially affect the outcomes of that work. Fairhurst and Sarr advise, "If issues are unnecessarily complex, simplify them. If there is misleading or suppressed information, set the record straight. If there are apparent discontinuities, forge linkages. If barriers to action exist, find new angles or remove or circumvent the barriers."

Painting the Big Picture

Several years ago on a trip to Amsterdam, we visited the well-known Rijksmuseum, home of some of the great paintings of the Golden Age of Dutch art, the seventeenth century. Among the paintings we saw was Rembrandt's famous "Company of Frans Banning Cocq and Willem van Ruytenburch," a painting better known as "The Night Watch." "The Night Watch," which depicts a group of militia in the moment just before they begin their march, is a huge painting, probably best viewed from fifty to a hundred feet back. It is an incredible painting in many ways, but one thing that stayed with us was the realization that, while the painting was best viewed from some distance back, Rembrandt painted it at arm's length. Each individual brush stroke was applied as Rembrandt stood only a foot or two from the canvas. Yet in some mysterious way Rembrandt knew how each of those brush strokes would contribute to the overall painting, what we might call "the big picture."

Another example of resolving the tension between close-up and distant perspective is, of course, Michelangelo's painting of religious figures on the ceiling of the Sistine Chapel. Considered some of the finest pictorial images of all time, Michelangelo's paintings were created while the artist was suspended on scaffolding high above the floor of the chapel. (Indeed, after working on the paintings for several years, Michelangelo's eyesight had been so affected that when he needed to read a letter or an envelope he had to hold it above his head!) Again, each of the hundreds of figures was painted at arm's length. Yet they are to be viewed from the floor of the chapel.

Isn't it amazing how an artist can keep in mind the overall impression that the painting is intended to convey and yet work on that painting through a series of hundreds, thousands, or even millions of individual brush strokes, many less than an inch long? It is remarkable, though we would say no more so than the fact that leaders face and have to resolve the same sort of problem. People talk a lot today about the leader's establishing a vision for the group or organization. While that is without a doubt an important function of leadership, we think that what is even more important, though less frequently mentioned, is the fact that leaders, like the great artists whose work we have just described, work at "arm's length." Their everyday activities involve conversations with people on the phone, meetings in their offices, conference rooms, or similar spaces, even chance meetings in the elevator or parking lot. Their work is up close and personal. It is immediate.

Yet everything the leader does has to contribute to the big picture. Each presentation, each individual conversation, each e-mail has not only to be consistent with the long-range image of what the leader is trying to achieve, it also has to actively contribute to the realization of that vision. Even if the vision of the group or organization is clear, the leader can't lay out all the individual steps that are required to accomplish that vision. Life is just too unpredictable for that. Chance and opportunity, fate and pure luck all intervene. So the best the leader can do is to make each "brush stroke" count, to make sure each individual move, each individual conversation, builds toward the ultimate accomplishment of the big picture. The leader has to be incremental and opportunistic, sensitive to the consequences that each small action will have for accomplishing the longer-term objective. In doing so, however, the leader has an opportunity to make a personal statement, an imprint on the history of the group or organization. As Jemeille Ackourey of the Boys and Girls Clubs of America told us, "You get to apply your own brush strokes. You get to add your own signature. You get to make it yours." In fact, you must.

Image-based Speaking

Leaders communicate differently in terms of what they say, but they also communicate differently in terms of the way they say things, specifically by using more frequent images, symbols, and metaphors to connect with human emotions. You may be familiar with this dramatic statement from Winston Churchill, master of the metaphor, warning of the impending threat of Nazi Germany: "I have watched this famous island descending incontinently, fecklessly, the stairway which leads to a dark gulf. It is a fine broad stairway at the beginning, but after a bit the carpet ends. A little farther on there are only flagstones, and a little farther still these break beneath your feet." Churchill, of course, could have used economic statistics or measures of the military buildup to make his point, but instead he spoke in images and metaphors designed to connect with people emotionally.

We suggest that part of what differentiates leaders from others is their more frequent use of such language. A leader's words are often most important because of their symbolic rather their literal meaning. Leaders often use metaphors, analogies, different rhythms, and even certain poetic devices to emphasize the symbolic content of their message. This tendency is probably most notable as you think about the major speeches of well-known leaders, but we suggest that the use of such language permeates the leader's conversation even in much less formal situations.

Interestingly, a recent study of the speeches of U.S. presidents sought to determine whether the propensity of presidents to use image-based language was related to the way they were perceived in terms of charisma and greatness. The findings of the study confirmed that the effectiveness of a leader's vision may depend on the leader's ability to paint a verbal picture of what can be accomplished by the group or organization. For these leaders, the ability to convey images in words was clearly linked with high positive regard by followers. "Leaders who use words that evoke pictures, sounds, smells, tastes, and other sensations tap more directly into followers' life experiences than do leaders who use words that appeal solely to followers' intellects."

In Table 4.1, we have listed a series of what are called "image-based" words and "content-based" words. In each pair, either

Table 4.1

Two Types of Language

Image-based	Content-based
sweat	work
rock	dependable
dream	idea
listen	consider
sweet	agreeable
path	alternative
grow	produce
journey	endeavor

Source: Adapted from Cynthia G. Emrich, Holly H. Brower, Jack M. Feldman, and Howard Garland. "Images in Words: Presidential Rhetoric, Charisma, and Greatness." *Administrative Science Quarterly*, 46 (2001): 527–557.

word could be used to express more or less the same sentiment. For example, Martin Luther King, Jr., could have said, "I have an idea." Instead, selecting the more image-based word for its greater emotional impact, he said, "I have a dream." Similarly, we could describe someone as very dependable or we could say they are "like a rock." The image-based words tend to connect more readily.

And, speaking of Winston Churchill, another example of how image-based words have greater emotional "staying power" is his famous phrase, "blood, sweat, and tears." What Churchill actually said was, "blood, sweat, *toil,* and tears." However, over time, history has "edited out" the word "toil" in favor of the stronger imagery of "sweat." ("Sweat" is a physical response that we experience when we engage in "toil," a more abstract word.) By using more image-based words, leaders engage others in terms of their life experiences and their reactions to those experiences. Image-based words tend to evoke sensory experiences, whereas concept-based words appeal more strongly to the listeners' logic and intellect. A lesson for leaders is to infuse your language with more image-based content and less concept-based content.

The best leaders have a tendency, perhaps a built-in tendency or perhaps one they have found to be successful in the past, to use more imagery than others, and that characteristic partially explains why they are perceived as leaders, why others follow. In our interviews of leaders, for example, we couldn't help noticing the number of times the people we were talking with used symbolic language or imagery to make a point. Jeanette Harrison discussed the events right after September 11 and her "experience of watching others execute under fire with grace." Lattie Coor painted a verbal picture of the "sweaty red brick buildings" at the University of Vermont, then when we asked about image-based language, he remarked, "It tells a story, doesn't it? As I think of those who have been effective, they do capture a visual thing. I describe it as the little executive summary in the front of our minds. I feel very strongly that we need to implant in everybody's little executive summary an accurate but hopeful and vivid image that shapes what people do."

In a similar fashion, Hugh Downs, who was chairman of the board of the United States Fund for UNICEF, shared with us his recollection of working with Chip Lyons, president of that organization. "When he was giving a report, it had to do with attention-keeping. Chip realized that you had to have images to keep people's attention. They aren't going to follow charts and graphs only. We should never lose sight of what we are about—the plight of children in the world. He really cared about the world's children and used images or word pictures to convey that." All of which is not to say that the message itself is meaningless or that only the emotion counts. But it is the use of imagery that seems to touch the emotions. Downs continued, "You have to have something that will engage and win the heart."

Physicality and Movement

Elaine Militello had just accepted a senior executive position with a top-notch marketing firm specializing in tourism, especially resort hotels. In her interview, she had been at her polished best and everything had flowed smoothly. But now that she had the job, she worried that her polished exterior would soon crack. Unlike her previous positions, her new job took her to a variety of locations, during which time she needed both to be very visible to those in the company (and outside) and to get acquainted with the people she would be working with. While she otherwise felt well prepared and excited to take on her new responsibilities, she worried about the fact that deep inside, she had always felt a little awkward traveling to new places and meeting new people. She was always afraid of tripping over "her own two feet," as her mother used to say, or somehow bumbling an introduction or a handshake. In fact, earlier in her career, she had been teased for being a "klutz," a reputation that was not enhanced by her generally haphazard appearance. While at the time she had almost enjoyed the good-natured ribbing, now she was worried that her awkwardness would hold her back. Her concerns were reinforced after she made her first couple of trips—she realized that people were not responding to her as he had hoped.

She asked her trusted friend Olivia Montgomery, a former dancer, for advice. Olivia urged her to work on her "image," but not just to get a new haircut and suit. Instead, Olivia told her that she needed to learn to walk more confidently, focusing on her posture and carriage, in the same way her dance instructor had taught her to enter a stage. "You know everything about this business," she told Elaine, "we just have to make the way you move on the outside of you match with how you think on the inside."

After a couple of months of practicing and trying to move carefully from place to place and meeting to meeting, Elaine had established an image as a polished professional in the eyes of others. With her friend's coaching, she moved well, she spoke well, and she even dressed well. In her own eyes, she was still very much on trial. She went back to her friend Olivia and confided that she still felt awkward. "I tripped over the carpet getting into the elevator the other day," she said. "I guess once a klutz always a klutz." Olivia reassured her that she was doing great, but, she said, "Don't take my word for it, just watch how people are reacting to you." As Elaine began to do so, she realized she was getting different reactions from the people she met. They were more attentive when she spoke. In fact, when she walked into a meeting, people looked expectantly at her, ready for her to "make a move."

Leadership is embodied; that is, leaders inhabit, use, and are limited by their physical bodies. Leaders don't just produce words (although the act of talking is certainly physical), they also gesture, vary their stance, use facial expressions, and move from one place to another. The way they use and move their bodies is very much a part of the message they communicate. Like dancers, leaders move their bodies through time and through space. Their work has a physical, even sensual dimension. Based on our conversations with dancers and choreographers, we are convinced that there is much more to the physicality of leadership than we currently understand. Certainly there is much more than the ordinary and even somewhat mundane descriptions of "body language" would suggest. Dancers and choreographers recognize much more clearly than do others the details of movement and the implications of movement. Dance innovator Doris Humphrey said: "The human body is the most powerfully expressive medium there is. It is quite possible to hide behind words, or to mask facial expression. But the body reveals. Movement and gesture are the oldest languages known to man. They are still the most revealing. When you move you stand revealed for what you are."

We're all familiar with the admonition to "walk the talk." But we suspect there's something deeper that resides in this statement than the way it's usually interpreted. Certainly a leader has to act in a way that's consistent with what he or she espouses, which is, of course, the typical interpretation of the phrase. But the leaders' actions also involve movement and, as Elaine learned, the movements may reveal a great deal. Literally, your walk has to be consistent with your talk. Or, to put it slightly differently, the way you walk has to be consistent with what you say. Especially at the highest levels, everyone watches the leader for clues to what's happening in the group or organization and what the future is likely to bring. People look to the leader and look *at* the leader to try to get some early indications of where things are going. People see what the leader does and then interpret the leader's intent through their own frame of reference. Some movements are likely to encourage people to follow. Others are not. In any case, the leader or potential leader is very much on public display.

This came up several times in our interviews. Tom Downs, former president of Amtrak, put it this way: "It's not what you say and it's not what you write and put out as organizational policy. It's what you do a hundred and fifty times a day. Everybody watches consciously or subconsciously what you do or don't do, how you react to everything. If you're uncertain or angry or frustrated or disengaged, it reads out." Similarly, former Fairfax (VA) county manager Robert O'Neill described the early days on a new job: "When I came here, you had to be 'on' all the time.

Every movement you made, every body twitch, everything was being interpreted by someone. There's a huge anxiety that builds up based on that. Once you've been there a while, the attention drops. Or at least you are not as sensitive to it."

The movement issue, of course, cuts in the other direction as well. By being sensitive to the physical makeup and movements of a group, a leader has another opportunity to connect with potential followers. Choreographer Liz Lerman told us, "I'm trained to look differently at how close or far people are, who's talking all the time, the tone of their voice, is their eye contact going through the room or caught in one area. Even within my small community you have to communicate differently with everyone you meet, because this new person comes in and they are going to bring their own stuff. You need to be responsive in different ways." The leader who understands the physical composition of the group, the specific rhythm that each person brings, the resulting overall rhythm, and the way movements are presented, will have special insight into the workings of the group.

That the physical composition of the group might affect its performance is obvious in the world of dance. Roy Kaiser of the Pennsylvania Ballet commented on that issue: "Some of the natural rhythm that dancers possess is dictated by their physicality. My company is a great example of this. I have this wide range of sizes and shapes. Each brings a different dynamic and different rhythmicality, naturally. There's going to be a more natural rhythm. Physicality can really dictate a lot." We suggest that physicality similarly affects the interactions of those in families, work groups, and organizations of all sizes. Any family experiencing the addition of another person—whether a new baby, a child returning from college for the summer, or a relative moving in to stay—recognizes that the sheer physical change has implications for all sorts of social interactions. Even in small groups, the relative sizes and body types of group members, their tendencies toward faster or slower movements, and their differing internal rhythms can surely affect the work of the group. The person who observes and understands these differences and then acts so as to complement and integrate these elements is more likely to be perceived as a leader.

We certainly recognize the idea of physical attraction between people, most obviously in the case of sexual attraction. But there is a similar relationship of attraction (or repulsion) that exists at many other levels and either encourages or prevents a sense of bonding between and among people. A significant part of this attraction or repulsion is based simply on the way people look and the way they move, their physical presence. We find some movement patterns or styles of movement more appealing than others and we might be drawn to follow someone with a particular pattern or style. "Movement is the connecting thread that allows me to join you in movement, dance the fear, and let you know that I too know about it, have been there and am here now with you," say Blom and Chaplin.

Some have even suggested that as individuals we develop particular patterns, styles, or approaches to movement that frame our moving from day to day and moment to moment. For example, one former dancer and student of movement analysis, Betsy Wetzig, describes four movement styles and associates these with personality preferences:

- Thrust—The "thrusting" pattern of movement and thinking is very direct and assertive, independent and critical, quick in pattern recognition, seeing the whole, and quite hands-on.
- Shape—The "shaping" type relies on seeing shapes or patterns, mostly logical patterns in the outside world. These people are concerned with knowing, with organizing, and "getting it right."
- Hang—The "hanging" style is more focused on energy and movement, engaging in associative or stream-of-consciousness thinking. This type can easily connect with everyone and is generally willing to "go with the flow" but also wants to "get going."
- Swing—The "swinging" pattern is more perceptive and playful, feeling oriented, and colorful. This type will be more indirect and meander toward solutions.

Some have argued, incidentally, that most major corporate managers have been thrusters, a type represented in dance by Martha Graham and George Balanchine, and in today's corporate world by Donald Trump and Martha Stewart. Indeed, Betsy Wetzig laughingly remarked to us that many corporate people move by "thrusting" forward what she called their "corporate rib."

For potential leaders, we suspect the issue is not trying to "model" one style of movement or another, but developing a clear understanding of one's own movement tendencies and how that style interacts with others. In terms of one's own style, we would suggest that those wanting to lead seek to fully understand their own movement style and how that style is most authentically grounded. Some have called this moving from one's center. According to Constance Schrader, "Learning to move from your center means learning to trust your own resources. As these centered movements come to you, you will realize that moving from your center is not only a fundamental movement experience, it is a fundamental life experience." In terms of how the leader relates to others, being able to work "across" various movement patterns is probably the central skill of the leader. The leader is probably the one who best connects with different movement patterns or styles, who, in a sense, transcends the diversity of movement styles.

Reprise

The issue of communication is extraordinarily complicated. Every word, every phrase we use is an interpretation based on our individual experiences as well as the accumulation of cultural norms and values that we come to hold as natural, inevitable. These are the parts of our presentation to the outside world that we don't question and don't even recognize as interpretations. For some, those we call "natural" leaders, a set of communication conventions significantly dependent on empathetic listening and evocative speaking comes naturally and seems to appeal to people, to cause them to follow. For others, those for whom such patterns are less natural, the capacity to lead is probably best enhanced by clearly understanding one's own predilections and perversities.

We think of leaders as speaking with energy and enthusiasm, with power and persuasiveness, engaging the moment and the audience. But the speech of a leader need not be passionate in its delivery; it doesn't need to be loud or insistent or strained. It does, however, need to touch the emotions of others. That is a matter of content, but also a matter of presentation style. For some people a more insistent style will touch the passions; for others it will extinguish them. At certain times one approach will be appropriate for the emotion of the moment. At other times, something else will be required. To know which is appropriate the leader must be able to sense the rhythm of the situation, and that, once again, requires a strong sense of empathy.

Moreover, the leader must also speak with clarity and authority, not authority in the sense of holding legitimate power to dominate or control others, but authority in the sense of confidence derived from experience or practice, self-assurance. We spoke earlier of the notion of rhythm as a coordinated flow of elements and we said that achieving such a flow of rhythm led to ease and efficiency in movement and relationships. Clarity in the leader's communications acts in the same way. Where the leader achieves ease and efficiency in his or her communications with others, people tend to react positively.

The most important lesson with respect to leader-like communication, we think, is that of achieving authenticity. The communication and movement patterns discussed in this chapter can be viewed simply as devices for persuasion, even manipulation. That is problematic from an ethical standpoint, but also, it simply won't work. People will see through a leader who is "faking it." Again, Hugh Downs was right on target in this respect: "The intellectual aspect may be manufactured. The emotional side cannot. You can only be yourself and you have to stand or fall on that." Leaders must have a vast reservoir of personal resources, including self-understanding, clarity and commitment, and occasionally the ability to laugh at themselves, in order to make the emotional connection with others that will allow acts of leadership.

5

Improvising with Creativity and Spontaneity

An executive points out the importance of being able to "act and think like a leader without having to stop and think about what a really active and creative leader would do in a situation like this."

Another comments, "I think the art of leadership is about having a plan, but not necessarily doing it exactly that way—being flexible about it. You have to know when to bob and weave, when to redirect the energy."

A dancer turned executive tells her people simply, "Improvise. Think on your feet. Change direction quickly."

In a commercial for the National Basketball Association, a fan screams, "That's what I love! It's improvised!"

One of the qualities that people most admire in an actor, a musician, or dancer is the ability to improvise. Audiences are moved, even spellbound, by Keith Jarrett's full-length improvised jazz piano concerts, and burst out in laughter over the impromptu comedy of Robin Williams. At its best, improvisation makes us sit up in our seats, our minds and hearts ready for whatever happens next. Improvisation occurs in a single moment, we become a part of that moment, and the energy and freshness of that moment capture both the performer and the audience with an immediacy of emotion that previously scored and rehearsed material cannot match.

This ability to improvise is, however, not only valuable to entertainers and artists. Leaders improvise as well. Indeed, a very high percentage of what leaders do is actually improvised behavior. You pick up the phone and are confronted by an unexpected problem, you follow the flow of conversation in a meeting and then react spontaneously to new ideas, you engage in impromptu hallway conversations about any of a thousand topics that might come up. While most leaders don't typically think of their work as improvised, or at least don't use that word, virtually all of the leaders we interviewed talked about the importance of being able to think on your feet, to respond quickly and correctly to questions that come up, and, generally, to act creatively and spontaneously in the moment. They spoke about the uncertainties of what any particular day or hour might bring and the need to respond appropriately. They told us about needing to speak rationally and carefully at times but also being able to speak from the heart at just the right moment. They spoke about the importance of staying fresh, full of energy and enthusiasm, and creatively meeting all the unplanned challenges and opportunities that present themselves over the course of a day.

Jane Hull, former governor of Arizona, certainly spoke of all of these related skills. She pointed out that leaders need to bring freshness to what they do. They need to give of an energy that shapes and directs the energy of others. "When you're on, you're on and you're never dragging. You have the energy and it has to project." One way to project that message, she advised, is to be able to prioritize, to know what's most important for any particular audience. "You may be addressing a group of legislators, meeting with business leaders, or talking with a group of educators. But in all cases you need to have a clear and powerful message. And you can't do that by spreading the message too thin. You need to get three to five major points and stick with those."

But, the governor continued, there's tremendous variety and flexibility in what comes up and you have to be ready for anything. There are always many unexpected things that happen in the course of a day, anything from an unexpected question from the press to a natural disaster. So you have to be able to think on your feet. "So much of what you do in leadership is go from crisis to crisis, or from goal to goal, or achievement to achievement. In any given day in a governor's life, there are at least three unanticipated crises, little ones or big ones." Interestingly, Governor Hull pointed out that one strategy for dealing with the current crisis was to be able to put "yesterday's crisis" behind you. One of her talents, she told us, was her ability to "cleanse the mind of what was there before." You have to be able not only to move from topic to topic, but to be fully prepared for the unusual, even the extraordinary, and that requires the capacity to improvise.

Improvisation is a vital leadership skill, one essential to the process of emotionally connecting with and energizing others. Improvisation may be, in fact, the best means to engage the hearts and imaginations of others. For most of us, what we say and do is largely controlled by our intellect. Our family socialization, academic and organizational learning have trained us and rewarded us for rationality, intellectual mastery, and control. Usually, this is appropriate and necessary in order to function and succeed in groups, organizations, and society generally. But, as we have already seen, taken too far, it can also be limiting and ineffective.

Improvisation, on the other hand, allows, even demands that we use all of our faculties at once—analytical, spatial, emotional, experiential, and physical—to produce what our intellect alone cannot. It allows us to draw from those things we know but cannot intellectualize. In this way, improvisation encourages us to do what we otherwise would not be able or willing to do. Improvisation requires that we bring forth our own creativity and spontaneity so that it is exactly suited to the particular moment and no other. Jazz clarinetist Pee Wee Russell once was given a complex and thickly notated musical composition and responded by saying that he could not play it. When he was then told that it was simply a written out version of an improvisation he had played the night before, "He still maintained that even if he could make sense of it, it would not come out the same way and it would be almost impossible to come even close to it without a great deal of practice." In leadership as well as musicianship, becoming a skilled and confident improviser enables us be more effective, more creative, and more "present" than otherwise possible. An improvised performance and only an improvised performance can be perfectly attuned to the moment.

How we respond to the world around us not only plays a

significant role in how personally effective we are, but also how others see us. If leaders or potential leaders fail to improvise, instead simply reacting to people and situations with routine, practiced behavior repeated over and over in the same way regardless of changes in themselves and the people they work with, their capacity for leadership will be diminished. Certainly taking this path requires the least mental energy. But it can also be stagnating, ineffective, and frankly, boring. People who take this approach are more likely to be seen by others as rigid, distant, and even inept. Such behavior is utterly inconsistent with the energy and enthusiasm associated with effective leadership. These people do not energize others; they are not viewed as leaders and others do not follow.

On the other hand, skilled improvisation on the part of a leader provides an important source of inspiration, guidance, and connection with others. People watch and listen to what leaders (or potential leaders) do in unguarded, unrehearsed moments. They gauge their own responses, emotional and otherwise, based in part on how the leaders act when something unexpected occurs. If leaders respond creatively, spontaneously, and with a good measure of grace to the people and situations they confront, they are more likely to be perceived by others as competent, engaged, caring, and flexible. They are more likely to energize others; they are more likely to be viewed as leaders.

Ironically, while improvisation is at the very core of artistic leadership, many of us might remain a little hesitant and uncomfortable with the word and its connotations. After all, improvisation to some may seem disturbingly close to "faking it." One wonders, in fact, whether the so-called imposter complex that many successful people experience—the feeling that "I'm not really good enough to do the work I'm supposed to do in this position"—might be related to the fact that confronting the improvisational aspects of our work is not something that is typically taught in school or written about in books. We imagine that others do not have to "make things up" as they go along (as we feel we are doing), and therefore we fear we are somehow less competent or prepared to lead. But improvisation is not a matter of simply "winging it." It is an ability that can be practiced and improved based on experience, skill, and expertise. It only looks easy. But as many important leaders have told us, improvisation requires knowing enough to let go and having the confidence and skills to trust yourself and the people you are with to see the process through.

Part of learning improvisation is to unlearn the barriers to creative and spontaneous improvisation that have been put in place over time. In fact, Keith Johnstone, who has taught theater improvisation for years, suggests that "Many who feel they are not creative have merely been damaged by their education." After all, a very strong argument can be made that all of us are born with a degree of creativity and with the ability to improvise; we simply need to rediscover it. Pablo Picasso is reported to have said at a children's art exhibit, "When I was the age of these children, I could draw like Raphael. It took me many years to learn how to draw like these children." In the same way, if you ask kindergartners if they can draw or make pictures, all will say that they can. If you ask high school students the same question, only a very few will raise their hands. Somehow over the course of our education and life experience, we lose our confidence in and facility for creativity and spontaneity. To be a successful leader, we need to reclaim that facility. Just as we have learned how to be rational, objective, and analytical, we can learn to be receptive, creative, and improvisational.

In this chapter, we draw from the world of art, music, theater, and dance to gain insights into the improvisational skills needed in leadership. We explore the sources of creativity and spontaneity in the process of improvisation. We consider how successful leaders have learned to improvise and how they feel about the role of and need for improvisation in the leadership process. Finally, we consider how to unleash and practice our own improvisational skills as well as those of other individuals, groups, and organizations.

The Elements of Improvisation

Chuck Kowalski was compulsive about preparation. For every staff meeting he conducted, he prepared voluminous notes, including not only the agenda but detailed comments about each topic that was going to be discussed. Every time he would move to a new item, he would take out a new folder and begin with the almost verbatim "speech" that he had prepared a day or two before. He also anticipated questions that might come up and either had an answer prepared or would put the question off until a later meeting so he would have time to put together detailed notes. He encouraged his managers to do the same, to be ready to speak from their notes on whatever topic came up. As a result, Chuck's management team meetings always seemed fully "scripted."

One Thursday morning in February, however, Chuck looked up at the clock and realized his management team meeting was scheduled at nine o'clock, ten minutes from now. And Chuck wasn't at all prepared. This was certainly understandable. His three-month-old child had been terribly sick over the past week and he and his wife had been spending countless hours at the doctor's office and even at the hospital. But, being the compulsive type he was, Chuck knew the meeting had to go on. He grabbed the single sheet of notes he had made on the agenda and headed for the conference room.

Members of the management team clearly took notice when Chuck arrived without his typical five-inch stack of folders, and while no one said anything, several members of the group quietly pushed their own notes toward the middle of the table or put them on the floor next to their chairs. Something special must be happening, they thought. Chuck opened the meeting, stumbled through an apology for not being as well prepared as usual, and asked for comments on the first item on the agenda, the location of a new plant. Several management team members reported on the review process and talked about a specific location in the Midwest they were most interested in. Chuck listened carefully, then heard himself saying, "You've clearly done a very thorough job of considering the logistical and financial issues involved here. But what about the question of whether our people would want to live in this place? I mean, it's pretty small, pretty remote, and, well, not very exciting." Someone at the other end of the table muttered, "You wouldn't catch me there." Chuck continued, almost surprising himself, "I mean, if we want this company to prosper we're going to have to be attentive to the quality of life we provide our employees, both on the job and off. Am I wrong?"

Chuck's long-time colleague and friend Ben responded, somewhat hesitantly at first, though he began to gain momentum as he spoke: "I think you're exactly right. We've been making good business decisions here for a long time, but I'm not sure whether our people decisions have always been that good." Someone else said, "Amen to that!" and soon a lively and energetic discussion of the issue erupted. Chuck chimed in himself several times, probably forgetting that he didn't have notes in front of him, and was pleased that his comments on quality-of-life issues seemed to be very well received. Several other topics were discussed in similar fashion before the meeting ended. As Chuck started toward the door, someone grabbed his arm and said, "Chuck, I just wanted to say: that was the best meeting we've ever had! Thanks!" Chuck smiled and thought, "Lesson learned."

Successful leaders have the ability to speak and work without a script, to act without perfect information, and to trust their instincts in the moment. When the pressure is on, they have the confidence to react with imagination and courage to situations as they unfold. They become skilled at improvising in the same way a highly skilled musician or artist or dancer responds to or interprets a situation or challenge in the course of a performance. "Leadership is an improvisational art. You may have an overarching vision, clear orienting values, and even a strategic plan, but what you actually do from moment to moment cannot be scripted."

In our interview, Bob Johnson of Honeywell Aerospace said, "You could take a strategy, you could develop tactics, you could decide how to tactically deploy them, and how to have a structure and how to staff it and what the metrics are. You could make a perfectly deployed detailed plan, where no thinking was required." Such a "scientific" approach to leadership would emphasize rigid adherence to a predetermined plan but would also remove human emotion and inspiration. The problem with that, Johnson said, is that "you'd have robots." People would just keep going even if the world changed, and that, he said, is the "enemy of the creative." Johnson concluded, "I think the art of leadership is about having a plan, but not necessarily doing it exactly that way—being flexible about it. You have to know when to bob and weave, when to redirect the energy."

If you think about someone "bobbing and weaving" as Johnson suggests, you might picture a tennis player standing in the "ready" position, responding from moment to moment as the ball is hit and bounces, sensing and redirecting the energy of a return, and ultimately shaping the outcome of the game through large and small adjustments. It is not a matter of just rationally calculating the trajectory of the ball; it requires sensing and feeling the rhythm of the volley, responding to all the environmental factors in play, and then allowing well-trained muscles to work. That does not mean that there is no plan or objective. Rather, it suggests that the ability to react, redirect, and change with fluidity and accuracy in response to the demands of the moment is ultimately what allows you to satisfy the plan and meet the objective. We thought Paul Bremer, U.S. administrator for Iraq, put it nicely in an interview when he spoke of "Strategic clarity and tactical flexibility."

The ability to improvise with skill and confidence is what allows leaders to respond to situations as they unfold, to interact with people as new issues and challenges emerge, to reach an audience in a particular context and time, and to continue to move in a desired direction even as the terrain changes. Organizational innovation has a clearly improvisational aspect. And, as we have seen, many writers have used the metaphor of improvisation in jazz or rock music to describe organizational innovation. But what if we think about improvisation as more than simply an organizational metaphor?

In jazz or dance, an improvised performance is one in which the details of the performance are not completely determined prior to the time of performance. But there is some planning and certainly some understanding that occurs. In other words, improvisation involves both preplanned as well as spontaneous elements. These planned and unplanned elements are held together by some sort of organizing structure or theme.

Think of a river that establishes the overall shape and direction of its waters; improvisation has been likened to the individual's movements that flow within and between the banks. The spontaneity and flow of improvisation is what gives improvisation its compelling, emotional quality. As jazz musician Sidney Bechet commented, "If you know in advance every note you're going to play and just the way you're going to play it, there's no need to have feelings. Like that, if you've got a feeling, you just can't use it; you can't even stay interested. Music like that, you could almost make a machine play it for you." It is interesting to note how similar Bechet's comment about machines playing music echoes CEO Bob Johnson's comment about robots following a plan. Improvising with creativity and spontaneity infuses the work, whether it be musical or social, with a freshness and energy that moves people.

Understanding improvisation in leadership requires attention to several points. First, improvisation is creativity within a particular structure, where some elements may be known and planned and others grow out of the situation as it unfolds. Second, it is the fusion of creation and execution based on expertise and skill. Third, in addition to expertise and intellect, improvisation evokes and is fueled by feelings and emotions. Each of these points is considered below in terms of their relevance to the experience of leaders.

Creativity within Structure

Artists, dancers, and musicians tell us that improvisation is based on a structure, with some rehearsed and some unrehearsed elements. It seems that in improvisation, creativity and spontaneity occur at least in part as the result of careful planning, preparation, and lots of practice. For instance, jazz performances are not usually purely ad lib: "An ability to improvise . . . depends, firstly, on an understanding, developed from complete familiarity, of the musical context within which one improvises, or wishes to improvise. . . . As this understanding develops, so the ability to improvise can develop." Certainly musicians understand the genre of music they are playing—jazz, rock, or bluegrass, for example. And they understand the basic melody and chord structure of the particular tune they are playing. Prior to a performance, they may even agree on an emotional theme or starting point. These ideas provide loose sets of tacit guidelines for the musicians to follow as they play.

The same is true in improvisational comedy. "Even improvisation groups like Second City have planned elements in their program. In each show, the actors have at least one set that they know has worked in the past." Improvisational comedians engage in what is called "priming." In those situations where the group is doing a set piece that only appears improvised, priming can be the same thing as rehearsal. But you can also prime for total surprises. In this case, priming involves building mental models based on one's background, experience, and personal values. It requires assembling the various elements you can draw from as the situation occurs. You prime or prepare yourself for spontaneity by anticipating the common features of the audience and the context and building routines around them.

From these planned elements, "Highly skilled players are able to retrieve the smallest fragments of patterns and, again with split second timing, combine them and recombine them in combinations in part or in whole with amazing continuity." In short, spontaneity in improvisation is based on what we already know. We can prime ourselves and plan and practice elements in a repertoire. But the strength of improvisation is that the expression of what we know is created and executed in a single moment, thus allowing us to throw aside our normal limits and to discover new and surprising and innovative ways of responding.

Like musicians and comedians, leaders also talk about the improvisational aspects of their work as depending on a particular structure and context. Improvisation requires preparation, and then a willingness to forgo a script. Judy Mohraz of the Piper Foundation, who also was president of Goucher College, told us that for her, "Improvisation is based on a core structure and variations on it. There is simply no way that you can or should script exactly how the dynamics are going to unfold in a complex situation. And while you have the under-girding of the goals that you want to reach, how you reach them will be variations on a theme." Leaders expect the unexpected, and plan for it. Alan Yordy, president and CEO of PeaceHealth (Oregon), also emphasized the need to be able to improvise as the situation unfolds, but at the same time to rely on judgment and knowledge. In his words, "I think the strongest leaders have an almost innate ability to improvise, to adapt, to be flexible, and to make very good judgments in a short period of time. I expect that every day is going to be full of unknown things. In today's complex and dynamic environment, those things are inevitable. You must view them as opportunities, then call on your judgment as to how to approach the improvisation."

Leaders from a variety of fields recognize that improvisation involves variations on a theme that occur in response to a particular audience or set of circumstances. They take what they know and what has worked in the past and then they put their hearts and minds in the "ready" position. They rely on "the plan" only to the extent it serves them and up to the moment it stops working. As they assess whether an approach is working, they are attentive to rational strategy, but also to those subtle changes in emotional tone, energy, and engagement that may create new opportunities and challenges. They expect to be surprised. But even as they try new things in response to these surprises, they don't abandon what they know. They try new variations, combinations, and recombinations of what has worked before. The effectiveness of these variations is dependent on the particular energy at play within a particular space and time.

Over the course of writing this book, we had an unexpected opportunity to test this idea in a series of speeches to various groups in Sweden. We knew that we would be talking about our work in a variety of areas including the subject of this book as well as the management of organizational change, building a culture of innovation, and the role of values in the leadership process. We also knew that we would be speaking together at six different venues for various periods of time. For a number of reasons, it was not possible to specify in advance exactly who and how large the audience would be or what the specific topics were or how long we would speak. We generally had little more than a few minutes in the car on the way to the meeting to plan what we would cover and in what order, how we would connect the parts, and how we would organize the material so that each of us contributed.

As we reflected on the experience, we realized that the lack of a script forced us be more attentive to the audience and to each other as co-presenters. We used different material in different ways for each of the six speeches. Each audience was unique. Some were larger and others smaller, some were more talkative and responsive, some participants were students and some were seasoned professionals. In order to connect with each, we had to sense and respond to each situation as it progressed. As a result, while elements of our presentations were prepared and rehearsed, the content and delivery was reordered, combined, and recombined in new ways each time. The transitions and connections we made had to be different in each context. When either opportunities or mistakes occurred, we tried to incorporate them and keep going. Because we were creating and executing the presentations at the same time, we felt able to connect more fully to the people we were talking with than if we had simply followed a preplanned speech. It is that sense of connection that is so important to the leader; improvising is one way in which it occurs.

Developing Skills and Expertise

In our interviews, artists and leaders often cited expertise, knowledge, and perspective as prerequisites to improvisation. In order to have the facility to create and assess variations on a theme, they said, you first have to be knowledgeable about the work at hand. Even before you prime yourself for creativity and spontaneity, successful improvisation requires expertise and experience with both the subject matter and the medium. That may be a bit surprising given the stereotypes many hold about improvisation as an exercise in "anything goes." Improvisation is not, however, simply random notes, steps, words, or brush strokes. In fact, it is the opposite. Improvisation requires more skill, practice, and mastery than the casual observer might guess. Yet it is fairly easy to recognize that improvisation without a firm foundation in skill and expertise is really not what most of us would call innovative or even aesthetically sound. We can pound on the piano, but that doesn't make it music. As art philosopher R.G. Collingwood stated, "First, learn to control your medium, to handle pencil and brush; then apply your skill to the problem in hand." It is the same in musical improvisation. First you must grasp how the notes and chords work together as well as the range and limits of your instrument. Then you can begin to play around with your own ideas. The best results are achieved when imagination and artistic expression are grounded in a firm foundation of knowledge, skill, and experience.

In groups, organizations, and societies, improvisation and innovation are built from experience and knowledge and tested with our intellect. The leaders we spoke with strongly confirmed this idea. Jeanette Harrison of Intel, for example, told us that "Improvisation is a refinement that requires a huge array of skill to draw on to even allow the latitude for improvising. Some improvise from lack of skill or lack of preparation and I don't think that is leadership. It's just covering up or masking ineptitude or lack of preparation."

The lesson with regard to knowledge and experience is simply this: the more knowledge and experience we can acquire the better, but once acquired, we have to see and work beyond it. We draw from it rather than rest upon it. Seen from this perspective, creativity depends on neither our imagination nor our intellect alone, but rather requires a conversation, even a dance, between them. David Miller, partner in Miller/Hull Partnership, the highly successful Seattle architectural firm, put it very well when he said, "Creativity occurs when we start conversations between the left and right brain." Knowledge and expertise form, in a sense, the stage upon which new ideas and fresh approaches can be developed and tried. Otherwise, we are just pounding on the piano.

When leaders and artists talk about knowledge as the foundation of improvisation, they are talking about a particular type of knowledge. How is this kind of knowledge acquired? The short answer is by paying attention. It is not enough simply to amass numbers of days and experiences; paying attention in this sense requires that we experience and learn from situations in a way that is deeper and more demanding than what many of us ordinarily do. Artists employ their experience in a way that allows them to integrate their perceptions with what they already know, and they allow this new knowledge to change them. As Celeste Miller of the Liz Lerman Dance Exchange told us, "The more things I can draw from at any given moment, the better that experience is—both emotional experience, historical experience, day-to-day experience, and movement experience. Knowing more makes me a better improviser." Artists emphasize the need to constantly seek out new sources of inspiration and ideas. Elysabeth Catbas of the Ballet Academy of Baltimore put it this way: "The more music you listen to, the more memories you have in your head. That adds to your creativity." But this involves far more than simply recognizing what music is being played. It is experiencing the music on an intellectual, physical, and emotional level that creates memories from which you can improvise.

Of course, the mere accumulation of new material is not always helpful. The new material has to be good material. We had lunch with the renowned jazz trombonist Vincent Nilsson, who has played with such jazz greats as Miles Davis and Dizzy Gillespie. He was making a similar point about gathering lots of music from different places, but, he pointed out, there are some times when you just don't want to hear certain things, waving toward the "elevator" music being piped into the restaurant. "Like passive smoke, some music infiltrates and you can't avoid it. That's like a pestilence you can't fight. But sometimes I can make a choice: is this something I want to have in my musical life?" Leaders also need to accumulate experiences but to some extent they need to be careful about what they "let in."

As we said earlier, learning from experience involves both left brain and right brain activities, sensing and intuition, feeling and thinking, aesthetic appreciation as well as calculating judgment. It uses all of our senses and faculties to gather information and to learn, not just intellectually, but with our whole selves. Some aspects of "paying attention" are discussed in other chapters. For example, listening empathetically and being entirely "present to the moment" are critical in this respect. The key is to absorb, reflect, and be open to experience as a way of enhancing not only what you do, but also how you act. Rather than simply cataloging the information in prearranged, rational categories, learning occurs on an emotional and even a physical level as well.

Learning in this way is not as mysterious as it might first appear. It is something that most of us do all the time, at least unconsciously. The task is to make all those levels of learning more conscious and deliberate, and therefore more usable. As theater instructor Roger Bedard told us, it is not really all that esoteric: "It's based in the ability to immerse yourself in the moment: none of this meta-cognition stuff. In other words, this is who I am in this particular situation and this is what is happening. And listening and hearing and moving forward." While Bedard was talking about training actors, successful leaders draw from their experience in the same way. Put in more concrete terms, giving twenty speeches provides experience, but paying attention and assimilating that experience allows you to feel and recognize moments that "worked" and to learn how it feels to connect and inspire. Becoming ready to improvise is far more than simply logging the miles. It is learning from the journey in a way that engages our minds and hearts, our intellect and imagination.

Part of the challenge is to be ready to draw from experience and to gain knowledge as the opportunity occurs. As already noted, the leader improvises within a given socially defined structure—the speech, the meeting, the corridor conversation. In each case, there is context that the leader must know, but the leader must also know how to operate flexibly within that context. With this understanding, the leader may be able to change the rules of the encounter, to restructure the encounter.

The only way to develop these improvisational skills is through experience. If something goes wrong, you have to keep going. The more times it happens, the more ready you are to improvise. You have to be flexible and willing to say, "This isn't working, let's try that." To do so requires mentally moving from one thing to another and being wholly open and present to both. If you are in a meeting with a particular group, you may gain any number of things from that interaction, including technical knowledge, insights into the interests of participants, information about how certain suggestions or actions were received, how well the group members interacted with each other, the rhythm and pace of their work, unmet needs and challenges, old problems and new ideas for the future, the level of trust and engagement, and so on. If you are then interrupted with a phone call, or go from there to an entirely different meeting or event, you have to leave the one situation in order to be ready to learn from the next experience.

We found our discussions with Dave Frohnmayer, president of the University of Oregon, particularly helpful in this regard. "Another attribute of leadership is the ability to change gears very rapidly, also a learned behavior. You may need to give an extraordinary concentration or focus to finishing a three-paragraph letter or memo of some kind, but there may be an unexpected interruption. You need to have the emotional facility to shift from one to the other and give it your full attention. You change subjects as well as audiences so many times in a day. Part of that is time management, but at some level you are going to be dealing with the unexpected. So you need the facility to change gears with as low an emotional pain as possible."

It is also important to emphasize that for these artists and leaders, useful experience is not simply the sum total of whatever happens to them. Rather, they are active in creating these experiences. They test ideas and thoughts, they question, they experiment, and they reflect on the results. Beyond that, however, they actually work to create opportunities for learning from whatever happens. One of the ways in which leaders and artists exercise this capacity of paying attention and acquiring useful experience is by consciously changing perspectives. New perspectives inspire and provide a vehicle for leaders and other artists and put new insights, information, and skills to work and provide ongoing sparks for further innovation. It is the mental equivalent to actually moving from place to place to gain new perspectives and insights. You try something, then move back to see how it looks from another perspective: "You go back and forth from the balcony to the dance floor. You take action, step back and assess the results of the action, reassess the plan, then go to the dance floor and make the next move."

These changes in perspective are critical to artists and leaders alike. Only by changing perspectives can they assess how individual actions and choices influence what happens immediately and up close, as well as how it looks and works from a vantage point that is farther away in time and distance. For example, Craig Curtis, partner in the Miller/Hull Partnership, told us that in working on the design of a building, he often finds himself "across the street." In other words, developing both the concept for and the reality of a highly functional and aesthetically interesting building requires attention to both the detailed drawings as well as the view from across the street. As we have already noted, having a sense of the "big picture" is important, but leadership is not defined merely by the splendor of the vision you convey; it's also how well you paint that vision in with individual brush strokes. Realistically, it is only the improvised details, the words we choose, the responses we give, the emotions we share from moment to moment, that any of us has to work with. The key is being able to change perspectives in a manner that allows you to see and assess what is happening from multiple perspectives at once. This allows you to create and improvise in a way that is unique and appropriate from a variety of vantage points.

Energy executive Bill Post summed up this point clearly and concisely when he told us that in his leadership experience, success is "one hundred percent action and communication, zero percent personal vision and intention. Makes no difference what my intention is; it makes every difference what people see me do." Post and other executives know that their work will be judged from a variety of different perspectives: now and up close, later and further away. Consciously changing perspectives is what allows leaders like Post to see how his actions and communications may "look" from varying distances and viewpoints and to evaluate the view over time. As we "paint" our vision at arm's length, we are constantly moving to see and evaluate how it looks from different angles and distances. As we experience and assess these differing perspectives, we change the next brush stroke.

Another way to think about perspective is to consider how differing perspectives can help us gain a sense of clarity. What may appear hopelessly complex and muddled from one angle or one distance, can take on a clearer focus and meaning or provide new direction from another. Judy Mohraz of the Piper Foundation, for example, in talking with us about the creative aspects of leadership said, "Through experience you become more educated, informed, skillful, but at some very deep level I think leadership comes from taking very complex patterns and complex issues and bringing about a kind of clarity." Such clarity, she said, can come from exploring problems, issues, and situations from as many different viewpoints as possible.

Evoking Feelings and Emotions

As already noted, improvisation is fueled by, and at the same time evokes feelings and emotions. Because improvisation can provoke feelings of fear and vulnerability, it requires confidence to do it well and keep it going. There is no avoiding the fact that improvisation can be risky business. John Corbett of the Art Institute of Chicago has written: "To improvise is to take the risk. Since the performer does not know for certain what will be played . . . the risk of failure, of complete collapse, is everywhere present." In part, it is this risk taking that makes the creative process exciting and exhilarating. But risk and potential failure are part of the process. As Larry Newman, world-class hang glider and balloonist told us, "I'd like to call what I do not just risk taking but creative risk taking. But the truth is, most of the stuff I've done has scared the hell out of me."

Part of the fear derives from the fact that improvisation makes us vulnerable to others. As we said earlier, one of the greatest values of improvisational leadership is that it allows us to connect emotionally with others. But this means that improvisation often results in showing a great deal of ourselves to others. Most unsettling, it not only can reveal what we know and don't know, it can reveal our emotions, our hopes, and our fears, all the things we feel most vulnerable about. The things we say and do when we improvise are often not as thoroughly filtered by our usual attempts to create a particular persona. Rather, they are an expression of who we actually are. Improvisation takes imagination one step further to demand that we act on our imagination and instinct in real time. That is a frightening prospect for virtually everyone.

Another reason improvisation can be unnerving is that you cannot be in a situation and then go off by yourself and consider all of the possible ways you could react before choosing a response. If you do, the moment is gone. Choreographer Kent Stowell told us that working through this kind of vulnerability is intrinsic to the creative process: "It might be personally risky or all kinds of things, but you have to trust yourself when you feel that you are trodding on new ground. The moment is fleeting. You take a break and it's shut down."

Many of the artists and leaders we interviewed talked about the vulnerability and fear of failure they feel when they improvise. But they also recognize that it is a normal and expected part of the process and that they simply have to develop the confidence to see it through. The key, according to General Ron Fogleman, is, "You have to believe in yourself." In other words, leaders learn to recognize the discomfort, accept it, and keep going. In fact, the nature of improvisation is that even if things don't go as you expect, you must keep going. As Andre Lewis, the artistic director of the Royal Winnipeg Ballet told us, the show must go on. Unexpected things happen; some good, others not so good. So he tells his dancers, "If you fall, please stand up. Don't walk off stage and say 'Let's stop the show.'"

Leaders find themselves in the same types of situations. They may be giving a speech to a group and recognize that the audience is not responding well. The most effective leaders recognize what is happening and try something different, rather than doggedly proceeding as if everything were going well, or worse, giving up and walking off the stage. Leaders find that in order to keep going, they must develop confidence in themselves and their skills to recover and maneuver and create as they go on. Judy Mohraz explained to us that it is in large degree a matter of becoming comfortable with yourself and the roles and responsibilities you have. She said it is not a matter of luck. Instead, she said, "You have to come to some self-realization that you really do have those skills. That gives you the confidence to do the improvisation that would have been difficult at an earlier age." Other successful leaders emphasized that the confidence needed is not based on the untried bravado of inexperience. Rather, they say, it is a more humble, mature sense of confidence developed over time by learning from both success and failure.

Another vitally important part of developing this confidence is self-knowledge and self-reflection. Put simply, because leadership improvisation runs the risk of revealing your "true self," it is wise to know yourself pretty thoroughly. Dancer and teacher Carol Press writes, "We create our understanding of others through imagination. This is the basis of empathy. Consequently, to be empathically aware of others, we must first be empathically aware of ourselves." While actors, dancers, and painters often talk about how their art involves confronting the very core of themselves and who they are, we were struck by how often creative leaders talked about the same phenomenon. They have looked inward with honesty and compassion, thought about their core values, and made a decision to risk being vulnerable to others.

It may be reasonable to ask, however, is improvisation worth the risk? Leaders agree that in groups and organizations, when important issues and values are at stake, the energy and exuberance that flow from improvisation make the risks worthwhile.

Vulnerability and failure are just parts of leading and inspiring people to do important things. Because that is the case, the difference between great leaders and the rest of us is that they develop the confidence to keep dancing. Artistic leadership is about reaching both the hearts and the minds of the people you work with. Doing so requires that you know your own heart and mind, be open to yourself and others, and be confident enough to take the necessary risks.

Fortunately, improvisation not only evokes feelings of discomfort, it also creates excitement and a sense of adventure. Artists and leaders must constantly work at "keeping it fresh" in order to create the excitement and inspiration they need in improvisation. As choreographer Paul Taylor said, "there's hardly anything when you're up (or down) a tree that's easier to hate than a . . . a systematic going-over of already climbed branches, especially if you've got a yen for adventure. Such a course seems distasteful so long as there remains hope for trying out new difficulties." Leaders and artists alike seem to relish the adventure. They work to find ways to draw energy and inspiration from the tension between the difficulties and possibilities. Perhaps Twyla Tharp, one of the world's best known choreographers, said it best: "I began to discriminate between fear and excitement. The two, though very close, are completely different. Fear is negative excitement, choking your imagination. Real excitement produces an energy that overcomes apprehension and makes you want to close in on your goal."

Artists are usually not thrill seekers. Rather, they are people who are energized by creative risk when there is a chance of making something better, more effective, more aesthetically pleasing, or whatever the case may be. Drummer and pianist Jack DeJohnette is quoted as saying, "That's what I like, the unpredictability of things. You run that risk when you improvise. You have to take those changes when they come and make something out of them, make something positive happen." In sustaining the energy needed for creativity and improvisation, keeping things "fresh" is essential; you need to introduce new material each time. "It doesn't only supply fresh stuff to work with, it imbues the whole performance with a spirit of freedom. It ejects what is no longer useful and revitalizes the remaining material."

Where does this fresh material come from? As discussed in the preceding section, the best leaders suggest it comes from opening themselves to and creating opportunities for new experiences. Beyond that, however, they seek out the unknown, the unsettling, and the unfamiliar to keep their creative edge and a sense of newness. They literally "refresh" themselves by discovering things about themselves and the world around them that they didn't previously know. They do unusual things and go to new places and read things they usually don't and talk to people that they haven't before.

Composer and jazz educator Steve Owen of the University of Oregon told us that he advises young musicians whose work is becoming dull and uninteresting to "Change environments—wildly different musical environments. The vocabulary you use in one is not applicable in another. If you find yourself being repetitive, change the environment, the music, or the musicians you are playing with." In a strikingly similar comment, health executive Alan Yordy told us that "taking enough personal time, through time away from the job, off time, down time, to stay fresh" was equally essential to artistic leadership. This involves "looking at other things, reading other things, being a well rounded person. As senior leaders we have an opportunity to buy additional time off. I encourage senior leaders to take as much as they can. Then on top of that I encourage senior leaders to take one or two days every year as a personal retreat, reflecting on something that has nothing to do with the technical aspect of your job, but has to do with the values of who we are, how we want to do things, how we want to function, and being fully self-aware. If you do those things, you're fresh and you don't get bogged down in this constant barrage of issues that can wear you down. So you have time to regroup, recharge, refresh, and that is most important."

In other words, in jazz ensembles and corporations, universities and ballet companies, government agencies and sports teams, there is a need to continually infuse the environment with new ideas, approaches, words, images, and actions. When leaders talk about keeping it fresh, they talk about the importance of continually bringing in new ideas and perspectives to challenge and engage people not only professionally but also personally. One of the things that can be helpful in this regard is, in fact, getting away from the situation itself. New and different experiences, settings, and interactions provide the fuel and inspiration for new ideas to emerge.

Leading Improvisational Organizations

Sara Rosenbloom had worked in accounts receivable for a computer manufacturing company for about fifteen years before abruptly moving to a highly successful marketing and public relations firm to handle their financial management division. While most of her work still involved what she liked to call "dollars and sense," she now interacted far more frequently with those on the more creative side of the house. Not only would she occasionally visit other parts of the company and see what people were doing on a day-to-day basis, but she was also involved in lots of meetings with her supervisor and with other division directors.

Sara was at first stunned by the free-wheeling, devil-may-care attitude that seemed to permeate most of the company. People tended to dress casually, except maybe on what they referred to as "Formal Fridays," and they spent lots of time standing around laughing and joking about the projects they were working on. As opposed to the more disciplined, even regimented feel of her previous work, here there was almost a playful attitude. Especially in staff meetings, she felt completely out of place. Privately she wondered, what kind of organization is this?

Finally, she had a conversation with a new friend at work in which she actually asked that question. The answer surprised her. "This is a very special place," he said. "In fact, it's really not like any other." He went ahead to explain that the company faced a different problem every day and so people had to be ready for anything. Moreover, most of the problems they encountered required a high degree of creativity and imagination in order to solve. "Jennifer [the president of the company] has actually worked really hard to create the atmosphere you see here—because she feels it's the one that will keep people sharp, flexible, and ready for anything." Suddenly it all came together. This wasn't complete chaos. Maybe it was "planned" chaos. But given the company's healthy bottom line, which Sara knew well, this approach not only made sense, it made dollars.

Leadership improvisation, or any other improvisation for that matter, is never completely solo. It requires far more than the most skilled, talented, artistic, visionary, and inspirational single person can ever provide. That is because improvisation combines the act of creation with the act of implementation in a social context. In dance, this can be likened to the process of taking the dance in the mind of the choreographer and translating it into the actual dance that will be performed on the stage. Septime Webre of the Washington Ballet talked with us about his creative process: "I find myself most creative from 9 to 11 at night with a stereo, two cold Mexican beers, and a composition book. I invent what the dancers are going to do." But that is not the end of the process, he explains. "The next day I'll teach them the steps. What they do might indicate a different way of doing it. We will abstract from the idea and improvise when we see what it looks like."

Improvisation not only occurs at a particular moment and in a particular context; it is also specific to one set of participants. A jazz riff played for one audience on a given night in a particular place will not be the same even if the identical notes are played at another time with another audience. In improvising, the leader is completely attuned to the participants in that improvisational encounter. In a very real sense, the leader doesn't simply respond to the participants, he or she makes them part of it. In this way, improvisation allows leaders to be at the right place, doing the right thing, at the right moment, with the right people.

Improvisation does not occur in a vacuum. The very definition of improvisation is that it requires the artist to simultaneously create and perform in a particular physical, temporal, and social context. Because creative improvisation occurs in the context of such an encounter, the quality of that encounter is influenced by the actions and reactions of all of the participants. In the same way that improvisation in a musical ensemble requires all participants to be skilled musicians, so does leadership improvisation require all participants to be both knowledgeable and skilled in the subject matter, as well as adept at engaging in improvisation. All of the members of a jazz ensemble lead and follow, all work together to simultaneously create and play the music. Good jazz, however, is enhanced by a room full of people who know and appreciate music and react with sound and movement of their own.

As we shift our focus from developing the capacity for our own improvisational skills to the challenge of a leader creating an environment where there are many skilled improvisational partners, some of the same lessons still apply, but they take on a slightly different focus. Leading a group or organization in a way that will enhance the members' own creativity and spontaneity requires attention to the same factors already discussed: developing expertise and knowledge, enhancing the ability to perceive and respond to ever changing situations, and evoking feelings and emotions. These skills and abilities are as essential to others in the organization as they are to the leader. The question here is, what can individual leaders, wherever they are in the world, do to facilitate the development of other creative and spontaneous participants?

As we have already suggested, improvisation does not require the abandonment of structure, order, skill, and discipline. The fact is that improvisation not only requires a structure, it thrives on it. Jazz flutist David Williams is quoted as saying, "Free improvisation is not an action resulting from freedom; it is an action directed toward freedom." In this way, "improvisation does not thus bypass power. They intertwine. I prefer to figure them as dancing rather than fighting, given that no one always leads and considering that no one will conquer." Improvisation requires structure in order to create a stage or foundation from which to proceed. In the world of dance, "by defining limits, by invoking a structure for the improvisation, what one is defining is ultimately a common ground for the dance to happen; it works toward achieving, for a certain space and for a certain time, a shared space, a space of co-habitation."

Structure is equally important to providing the basis for improvisation in groups and organizations. The reason is simply this: if everyone is going to have a chance to be creative, structure is the only thing that keeps the interaction from becoming a chaotic mix of participants each seeking their own freedom, even at the expense of others. In order to provide for aesthetic or creative freedom, the structure must assure that there is not domination or restriction by one participant over others. Structure then provides the participants with the freedom to move within limits, a constraint that in the final analysis provides more freedom of movement than would be possible in an improvisational free-for-all.

This is particularly important because, as we discussed earlier, improvisation involves risk and vulnerability. For people to participate, they must first and foremost feel safe that they (and their ideas and contributions) will not be shot down, put down, or pushed down. Most of us know the rules of brainstorming—no interrupting, no criticism, give ideas in order around a circle—but the importance of these rules becomes clear when we recognize the emotions and fears inherent in the act of improvising. These rules ultimately create a feeling of safety, and therefore freedom among the participants. What's more, when the participants test those limits and find that they will be enforced, it ultimately creates even greater feelings of trust and confidence. Without such trust and confidence among the participants, improvisation will be short lived if it emerges at all.

In the same way that creativity must have a structure to flourish, groups and organizations require rules, limits, boundaries, and constraints in order to be most creative. Robert Lowe, in his book *Improvisation, Inc.*, in fact likens the bonds and interactions between people in an improvisational setting to a community. "The Improv itself," he writes, "is composed of values that create strengths of community among people participating. The practices and principles of improvisation create strengths of communication among the people playing." This is a highly useful metaphor for the type of environment needed in groups and organizations so that creativity and spontaneous improvisation can flourish. People must know, trust, and rely on one another. For the "community" to work, the members need to feel part of a larger whole and committed to the values of the whole. One of those community values should be that risk taking will not be punished and that failure will be treated as an opportunity to learn. Even better, the community can hold as a shared value the importance of celebrating and supporting creativity and spontaneity.

As already noted, in addition to the rules and structure necessary for mutual respect and the freedom to create, improvisational skills also rest on a foundation of knowledge and expertise. From the perspective of trying to build an improvisational community, it is important to recognize that participants need to be trained in the process skills of improvisation, they must also be highly trained, qualified, and current in their substantive area, just as jazz musicians need to know and master their instruments before they improvise. So there are two sets of knowledge and skills needed: the first are the substantive expertise and skills involved in that particular job or profession, the second are the process skills that allow people to interact in an improvisational setting.

All of this suggests that to build a group or organization with many skilled improvisational partners requires a significant investment in time and training. It is not enough to simply walk in and expect people to be able to improvise appropriately and skillfully. It is a matter of recognizing that each project, each interaction, each speech, each gesture, and each decision is an opportunity to either enhance or denigrate those individuals' future capacity for improvisation. If people are excited about a project, are they allowed to run with it in order to learn from mistakes and build confidence? Are they given the time and training and freedom to gain mastery in their area of expertise? Are they given the opportunity and the charge of knowing their organization as a whole and the values it represents? Only if so will they have the experience, confidence, and expertise needed to be good improvisational partners.

From the perspective of the leader working to build an improvisational organization, the key is to start wherever you are with whatever is in front of you. If given a firm and consistent foundation on which to grow, the capacity to improvise will build with time and practice. In tension with this need to provide structure and a foundation of skill and trust is the requirement that you then allow people the freedom to be creative.

By necessity, this freedom requires that we allow people to both succeed and fail. The goal is not, however, to avoid failure. The goal is to teach people to watch themselves, to be self-reflective, and to learn from trial and error. In the long run, it may be less important that an individual project succeed than if the people involved are left more capable of succeeding in the future. Dance educator John Wilson told us that in dance improvisation the goal is to get people to watch themselves and evaluate what they are doing: "The purpose is to approach whatever form you do with a greater ability to interpret." In other words, improvisation depends on the ability of the person to understand how well they are doing, as they do it—and to make adjustments accordingly. People will not develop this capacity if the evaluation is only external. The ability can be fostered by actively asking them to talk about and evaluate not only how what they did felt, but also how it worked and didn't work in a particular time and context.

People learn to improvise by improvising. In the same way that you cannot get in physical shape by watching others exercise, the only way to learn to improvise is by trying it and practicing it. Moreover, you cannot force people to be more creative or to practice improvisation. What a leader can do is to work on his or her own improvisational skills, create an environment and opportunity for others to involve themselves in the improvisational process, and to be ready to engage with them when they do. From this point, improvisation builds on itself, sparking energy and vitality and creating connections between people in a way that makes virtually anything possible.

Reprise

Improvisational skills are vital to the leadership process. Improvisation is what allows leaders to respond to situations and opportunities as they occur with both sensitivity and a sense of shared purpose and direction. The ability to improvise is based on thoroughly knowing the subject matter and the context, and gaining sufficient expertise to build confidence and self-assurance. Improvisation consists of elements that are known and unknown, allowing the leader or artist to draw from familiar material and combine and recombine, create and execute simultaneously. Priming or practicing this material allows new variations to emerge. All of this requires experience, but this experience is not just the aggregation of hours and years. Both artists and leaders who become skilled at improvisation seek to use and be open to their experience on an intellectual, emotional, even physical level. They allow, even invite those experiences to change them. In some sense, they almost seem to collect experiences as a future resource to build from and play with.

Artists and leaders also tell us that changing perspectives, thinking from different angles, and viewing situations from different distances provides them with new ideas and insights. They pay close attention to those around them, moving from moment to moment and focusing on each as it occurs. They speak about the courage and confidence that it takes to improvise, but also about the excitement it generates. For them, the risks of improvisation are outweighed by the energy it spawns. To maintain this energy, they talk about the need to stay fresh, to actively and consciously try new ideas and approaches, change scenery, and test themselves and others in new environments.

In building an organizational context that fosters improvisation, leaders must recognize the need for adequate training so that people are able not only to gain expertise in their subject area but also to become skilled in improvisational techniques. They can be taught improvisation by practicing it, priming for events, and working with others in a creative and innovative environment. Through practice, people can learn to be self-reflective and more aware of others, thereby gaining both the expertise and the confidence needed for skilled improvisation. Crucial to the process is to create a community that is structured by rules of conduct and based on the values of trust and mutual respect. People must be given the freedom to try and the opportunity to fail in a context that provides sufficient safety for them to learn and build from mistakes. Over time, the ability and willingness to improvise can spark new energy and creativity in organizations and groups, and forge bonds of trust and community.

6

Leading from Within

What makes the difference between good dancers and great dancers? It's not technique; it's focus and concentration. As one dance instructor put it, "Just having a taller ladder gets you to the roof, but it can't get you to the moon."

A major corporate executive confesses that many of the most important decisions he made in his career were more a combination of confidence and good luck than planning and analysis.

A highly successful entrepreneur laments the fact that "You have a dream and everybody wants to steal it away from you. They try to take it away from you by saying things like, 'Why are you doing that? It's silly.'" He recommends that you just move ahead.

The vice-president of a leading computer company tells us, "There is a sense of integrity, of honesty, that when you are put to the test, you have to answer. There is part of that personal cloth of who you are as a human being that shows most clearly then."

Several times we have mentioned the fact that both dance and leadership occur "in the moment," then are gone forever, remaining only in our memory. While poetry, sculpture, architecture, painting, and writing are available as finished products to which an observer can return, dance, drama, music, and leadership can be accessed only in the moment. As choreographer Merce Cunningham remarked, "Dance is concerned with the single instant as it comes along." For this reason, there is a sense of immediacy in dance and leadership that is lacking in other arts.

Dance and leadership take place in the moment, yet that moment and those that follow it are ones filled with meaning. Through these connected but ephemeral moments the dancer or leader must communicate something special, something that connects with the audience and causes them to respond with emotion, insight, or commitment. Dance and leadership are both momentary and fleeting, yet they can have great impact. But only if they bring forth the total education and experience, ingenuity and artistry of the dancer or leader. It's as if there is a lifetime of preparation compressed into a single instant.

In that moment, the artist may connect emotionally through the use of certain techniques or skills, but these only form the base upon which the real drama unfolds. Broadcaster Hugh Downs used an interesting metaphor to make this point: "You need a carrier wave. In radio, amplitude modulation radio (AM), works by way of a very high frequency radio wave, called a carrier wave. But imposed on that is a sound wave. Without the carrier wave, nothing will go across. The carrier wave is the ability you have, the technique. Superimposed on the carrier wave there can be a very artistic way to say the words. You've got to have something to put on it, a broadcast that means something. You've got to have a technique on which you impose something that is almost mystical."

The artistic leader, as we have seen, has a variety of skills and abilities that he or she uses and that have the effect of creating a sense of emotional connection and stimulating people to move in a new direction. The leader needs to understand the rhythm of the group or organization; the leader needs to be able to improvise with creativity and spontaneity; and the leader must understand how to communicate in images, symbols, and metaphors. But beyond these elements of skill that constitute the leader's "carrier wave," the leader, like the dancer, has to call on a variety of inner resources that are essential to his or her artistry.

Those inner resources are the subject of this chapter, but discussing them is difficult because they contain such interesting and complex contradictions. Again, the world of dance is instructive. Septime Webre of the Washington Ballet talked with us about one of the most fascinating contradictions in dance—the fact that in order to reach the highest level, the dancer or choreographer must be extremely focused, disciplined, and dedicated to his or her work and, at the same time, be highly creative, spontaneous, and artistic. These are two quite different sets of skills, one tending toward order and convergence, the other toward disorder and opposition. Yet both are needed for the dancer or choreographer to be successful. The dancer or choreographer must engage in extraordinarily difficult work and have the discipline to stay with that work even under the most trying circumstances. He or she must also demonstrate extreme creativity, the creativity of shape and pattern and movement.

There is a related contradiction we have already noted: that between structure and creativity, or between planning and spontaneity. While these characteristics seem at odds with one another, there must exist a certain structure for dancers to follow (at least in most dance forms). At the same time, there must always be room for interpretation and self-expression in order for the dance to remain fresh and engaging. We asked dancer and choreographer Ron Brown about how much of his work is choreographed and how much is improvised. He responded: "It's all choreographed, but dance is in the moment, so it feels different every time." Approaching the contradiction from the other direction, however, we recognize that while it is important to allow for creative expression, the structure of the dance, including both its genre and its choreographed movements, sets limits beyond which the dancer or choreographer cannot go and still be taken seriously. The individual who is obsessive in terms of discipline may be considered rigid and overwrought; the creative individual who knows no limits may be considered erratic or even hysterical. The artist must reach just the right plain of commitment and creativity without going beyond the limits that the structure of the dance permits.

The same is true of leaders, especially those who lead at the highest and most visible levels. Leadership is hard, hard work. It requires an enormous capacity for focus, discipline, and commitment. At the same time, the leader is expected to exercise a certain creativity and artistry, not the same kind of artistry as the dancer or choreographer, but artistry with respect to bringing the right people together at the right time, drawing forth a vision of the organization, saying just the right words to stabilize or mobilize the group or organization, and establishing a flow of energy in the direction that is selected. The leader need not *necessarily* be creative with respect to the substantive work of the group or organization, although the leader's good ideas contribute just as do those of others. And, of course, a person perceived as creative may instill confidence among others and connect emotionally in that way. But the leader must be an artist with respect to human energy, especially that energy expressed in human relationships.

The leader must also stay within the bounds of the structure within which he or she works. Different situations impose different structures or limits. It will probably be inappropriate for the member of a small group or team to give a long-winded speech from behind a podium, no matter how eloquent it might be. On the other hand, the leader of a large organization sometimes has to rely more on speeches to large groups than on individual conversations with everyone in the organization. The leader has to have a clear understanding of just how far he or she can go and still be believable within the context in which they work. Phil Fulmer's use of the "synergy stick," for example, probably stretched the limits of what a football coach can get away with, but it remained within those limits. We also suggest that expectations with respect to the balance between discipline and creativity would be somewhat different in the military or on the flight deck from those in a school or an art museum.

Focus and discipline may often contend with creativity and artistry, but both must be available to the leader. In this chapter we will discuss both the "inner disciplines" and the "inner resources" we consider necessary for artistic leadership. Our discussion of the inner disciplines will include attention to focus and concentration; hard work, passion, and discipline; and a curious blend of confidence and humility. Our discussion of the inner resources will include attention to making meaning and effecting change. In either case, we think it appropriate to view this cluster of ideas as constituting a capacity for "leading from within."

The Inner Disciplines

During the course of our work on this book, we witnessed a number of marvelous dance performances, but none stands out more clearly in our memory than a rehearsal of the Washington Ballet that we attended. We had interviewed Septime Webre, artistic director of the ballet, over lunch, after which he invited us to join him and his dancers for an afternoon rehearsal. We enthusiastically agreed and soon found ourselves in a large studio, about the size of a performance stage, with Webre, the rehearsal director, and about fifteen to twenty young dancers. We noticed immediately that nearly all of the dancers were wearing at least one bandage somewhere on their bodies, typically on an ankle, a wrist, an elbow, or a knee. And as they began dancing we saw something that you never really see sitting in the audience at a performance, that is, what incredibly hard work they were doing. We could see them sweating, we could hear their gasps for breath, and we could feel the impact when bodies came crashing together.

After an hour or so of large-scale company productions, they came to a piece choreographed by the brilliant Singaporean choreographer Choo-San Goh, who had been resident choreographer at the Washington Ballet but who died at an unfortunately early age. A young man and a young woman began with a beautifully lyrical segment, building in intensity until she was in the front right of the stage and he was in the back left. She ran full speed diagonally back across the studio and leaped headlong, arms outstretched, into his grasp. They continued their amazing performance to its conclusion.

Something early on in the piece had not been all that they desired, so they decided to go through the piece again. They started slowly, then once again they got to the point where she was in the front right and he was in the back left. Again, she ran full speed and leaped into his arms. But this time something went wrong. No one was sure exactly what happened—perhaps his elbow hit her ribs—but she simply crumpled in a little ball on the floor. Others rushed over to help, asking repeatedly what was wrong. She just lay there for what seemed like an eternity. Finally, she began to move, ever so slowly. With the help of others, she got to her feet, though still not able to stand fully upright. Someone asked if she could stretch and she slowly, very slowly began to raise her right arm. She had only reached the point where her hand was about even with the top of her head, when someone said, "Okay, let's do it again."

To our amazement, she and her partner immediately went back to the beginning and started through the dance again. They completed the early, more lyrical part, then got to the point where she was in the front right and he was in the back left. This time, we are convinced, she ran faster than either of the other two times, made her leap . . . and he caught her. At the end of the piece, everyone in the room burst into applause. That afternoon, we learned what dedication is all about.

Focus and Concentration

When we asked dancers and other artists what makes the difference between the good dancers and the great dancers there were generally two answers, one we expected and one we didn't. As we expected, many answered that the truly great dancers had a certain *presence* on the stage that others lacked. They had incredible technique; that was a given. But there are some dancers who are incredibly talented, but have nothing going on inside. The very best dancers have the ability to connect emotionally with the audience.

Robert de Warren of the Sarasota Ballet has worked with some of the greatest dancers of our time and made an interesting comparison between Rudolf Nureyev and Mikhail Baryshnikov. Both, he said, had amazing technique; however, in his view, Baryshnikov was even stronger, had higher elevation, and more of everything. "But," he said, "you couldn't compare the two personalities artistically because of the extra something." The presence that Nureyev exuded on stage was special. "The athletic side is wonderful and challenging, but if you have the other side that touches your sensibilities deeply, that's where you get the real big important artists." So one difference between good dancers and great dancers is their presence, their ability to connect emotionally.

The other difference our interviewees talked about, the one we found somewhat surprising, had to do with focus and concentration. Martha Graham stated this point well when she said, "To me, this acquirement of nervous, physical, and emotional concentration is the one element possessed to the highest degree by the truly great dancers of the world. Its acquirement is the result of discipline, of energy in the deepest sense. That is why there are so few great dancers." The great dancers have the capacity to focus completely on what they are doing. They are right there, completely there, in the present, in the moment.

Dance educator Joann Browning of the University of Delaware was the first person we heard use the phrase, "Be present to the moment" in relation to dance, though we heard that phrase used over and over in our interviews. While you are dancing there are a thousand things that can be running through your mind. Some are completely extraneous to what's going on, like "I wonder what I'll have for dinner." Others are forced on you, as related by a dancer who told us about the time she ran into a light boom in the first piece of the evening. Later, "In 'Dying Swan,' all I could think about was, 'I hope they can't see the blood.'" There is also a temptation to think about the dance itself, to analyze what you are doing as it occurs. To some extent that is inevitable, especially if you are dancing with others and must remain constantly aware of where you are in relation to those others.

But dancers caution against overanalyzing. Alcine Wiltz of the University of Maryland put it this way: "If you're aware that you are thinking about what you're doing, then you're not dancing. You're only analyzing." At some point dancers have to allow their training and experience, their endless practice, their muscle memory to just take over. Champion figure skater Scott Hamilton, during his broadcast of the 2002 Winter Olympics figure skating championship, told about the advice someone gave him just prior to his own gold medal performance. His friend said, "Skate stupid," meaning that you should empty out the running dialogue in your head and just do what you know you can do on the ice. Yogi Berra also put it simply when he said, "How can you think and hit at the same time?"

There is a time for thinking (analyzing) and a time for acting (or dancing), but you have to keep the two separate. Golfers are especially susceptible to the dangers of overanalyzing. The golf swing can be analyzed in great detail and most golf instruction focuses on just such analysis. But if the golfer allows multiple "swing thoughts" to come into his or her mind during the swing, the swing will likely break down. Jim and Ceci Taylor, writing in *The Psychology of Dance,* discuss the same issue with respect to dance:

> There is a time and place for every aspect of the dance experience. For example, class and rehearsal are the appropriate settings for you and your dancers to analyze and critique their dance. However, when it is performance time, it is no longer suitable to question, doubt, analyze, or think about technique. Unfortunately, excessive cognitive activity, called jamming, results in a decline in self-confidence, an increase in anxiety, and poor execution of the required skills. Rather at this stage, dancers must set aside these concerns and trust their ability to perform the best they can, letting the learned sequences of skills emerge automatically and without conscious control.

There are several reasons why dancers are urged to "be present to the moment." One is that if you are not focused on the moment you will lose your place. "If you're in a dance class, you can't let your mind wander. There are three of these and four of those. If your mind wanders, you'll fall down." You can't maintain your competence without being attentive to the moment. A second reason to "be present to the moment" is that if you are mentally somewhere else, the audience will sense that and you will lose your connection with them. Only when the artist is fully focused on the role and the performance will the audience's attention remain there as well. Few things turn someone off emotionally as easily as their being ignored—and if the dancer is somewhere else mentally and psychologically, he or she is ignoring the audience. A third reason to "be present to the moment" is that when a dancer's technique is so engrained that they are able to let go, it often permits something really spectacular to happen. The subconscious comes into play and the emotional energy that we talked about earlier moves to the fore.

Here, the two ways in which great dancers are distinguished from good dancers come together. The dancer's "presence" is enhanced by "being present." Joann Browning talked about these two elements of artistry as if they were one. While she cautioned against discounting skill or technique, she argued that for her students, at a certain level, their technical skill just can't take them any further. You have to create openings in which students can discover a sense of artistry so that they can convey feelings through movement: "They need a new paradigm. Just having a taller ladder gets you to the roof, but it can't get you to the moon." Technique is the ladder, but it takes the combination of "presence" and "being present" to get you to the moon.

The leaders we interviewed easily recognized the importance of focus and concentration in their work, and some even used a variation of the dancers' phrase, "being in the moment." All put the issue of focus and concentration in the context of the many issues pressing for the attention of the leader, especially one at the top of a large organization. George Fisher of Kodak put it this way: "As a leader, you have to juggle a ton of things—twenty, thirty, maybe even a hundred a day. But at any given moment you have to be totally focused on what it is you're dealing with. If you have thirty things to do in a particular day and you are working on number three, you can't be thinking about any one of the twenty-nine other things. You've just got to be zeroed in. On any one of those tasks you have to give it 100 percent of your attention. I can't remember an important discussion when I was thinking about anything else. I've been in boring presentations where I thought about something else. But on an issue that I'm dealing with, Rome could be burning over here, and I'd be right there."

Astronaut and space shuttle commander Charles Bolden used the term "compartmentalization" to describe the way he thinks of things in separate boxes, so that he can concentrate fully on what's important: "You've got to focus on the mission or whatever we're trying to do here. You have to 'compartmentalize,' jump into this box that is the moment, what's going on right now, what's the mission. When you get on your motorcycle, you've got to stay focused. You want to enjoy the scenery and everything else, but you've got to remember you're on a motorcycle." Bolden pointed out, however, that sometimes you at least need to be cognizant of what's going on around you, just outside the box. There's a lot that you have to be sensitive to, but you have to sort out what is relevant to the mission and what is not, what to bring in and what to leave alone: "The leader has to have the peripheral vision to see all this stuff that's going on but not be distracted by it."

Former governor and U.S. senator Daniel J. Evans made a similar point with respect to the political arena: "You have to focus on what you are doing but also on what everybody around you is doing. A political leader keeps the focus on the end result, but in trying to get there keeps making sure that all the other people involved in the effort are doing there job. Focusing on the end result may mean calling a couple of legislators into your office to change their mind or asking them what it would take to change their votes." In making the point that leaders need to keep their eye on their objective and not get lost in the details, Evans's analogy was a chess game: "There are a lot of chess pieces on the board but if you get lost in the maneuvering you probably will lose the end result. The focus has got to be on your goal."

In part, the need for focus and concentration derives from the rapidity of social and economic change that so affects major organizations in all sectors today. Under these conditions, the leader cannot be just a bystander, but must be very much engaged and in the moment. Bob Johnson of Honeywell Aerospace used a clever analogy in talking about how the CEO has to be sensitive to the rapidity of change in business. He said, "I had a Ferrari for a while. When you're going 160 miles an hour, you gotta be there. You don't want any music on, and you're not smoking, and you're not talking. You gotta be there." The leader has to be paying full attention to everything that is happening. If there are lapses, the Ferrari can wind up in a ditch.

In some ways our technological age has made it more difficult to maintain focus and concentration. How many times recently have you been talking on the phone with someone and, while the conversation was continuing, you started to check your e-mail? The person on the other end doesn't need to be a genius to figure out what's happening—they hear the clicking and they realize that you've lost the "rhythm" of the conversation. And they are likely to be frustrated by being ignored in this way. If you are not going to stay fully with that person during a phone conversation, it's very unlikely they will see you as a leader. They may respect your managerial capacity to "multitask" but the emotional connection needed for leadership will have been broken. (Incidentally, one workshop participant told us that in order to avoid being distracted by e-mail or even notes or documents on his desk, when he talks on the phone he stands up and looks out the window.)

The technological issue has also crept into the boardroom, but at least some executives are sensitive to its possible effects. Alan Yordy of PeaceHealth suggested that leaders need to be able to shift topics quickly, but also stay on topic: "In order to be fully effective you have to be in the moment. We are a heavy user of e-mail in this organization. In meetings, everybody has a laptop and they are all plugged in. What we find happening in these meetings is, as we deal with different topics, different people will be doing e-mail. We've developed a ground rule that for certain subjects the computer lid goes down, because you have to be in the moment. You have to be focusing on what's being said and what the issue is if you're going to be fully effective." Leaders would be well advised to work on their own capacities for focus and concentration, but also to make sure others are being "present to the moment" as well.

For the leader, there are important reasons to maintain a high degree of focus and concentration. One is to maintain a sense of competence. If you are drifting away you won't be able to perform at your best and your mistakes will likely show. A second is to maintain an emotional connection with those around you. If you are fully present in every conversation—and indeed if that becomes a habit—people will respond in a positive sense emotionally, something that we think is essential to the act of leading. Incidentally, in each of the many interviews with leaders we did, we were probably the least important item on the leader's agenda that day. Yet consistently these leaders were absolutely present in our conversations, showing no evidence of wondering what was next on their calendar or who might be waiting outside. A third reason to maintain a high degree of focus and concentration is that sometimes doing so can lead to real breakthroughs in your performance. Just after Olympic figure-skating champion Sarah Hughes finished the incredible performance that resulted in her gold medal in Salt Lake City, she remarked, "I did things out there I can't do!" It is very likely that it was her complete focus and concentration that allowed this.

Ronnie Scott, the British jazz musician, commented on the special feeling that accompanies such a performance. "It's a certain feeling you're aiming for—or unconsciously aiming for—and when this happens—inspiration—duende—whatever you like to call it—a happy conjunction of conditions and events and middle attitudes—it will feel good. It will feel that 'I should be what I am' kind of thing." A city manager in a small Kansas town once told the story of a group of business people who came to town to explore the possibility of locating a plant there. After their conversations at City Hall, they adjourned to an old railroad car turned into a restaurant. After dinner, the manager got up and, as he put it, "did his thing." He later reflected, "Bob, I was so good that night. *I was better than I know how to be.*" Sometimes focus and concentration, being present to the moment, can make us better than we know how to be—and that feels really good.

Hard Work, Passion, and Discipline

Being a dancer is hard, hard work. Agnes de Mille, choreographer for both ballet and Broadway, said, "A dancer . . . who fears or dislikes work and failure should get out immediately. It's extremely hard work and if you don't take joy in it too, if you're not excited and inspired by it, it's not for you." Dancing, especially at the highest levels, is a physically and mentally demanding occupation, requiring hours and hours of exhausting athletic moves, the ability to withstand and work through pain, and constant attention to what you eat and drink so that you can be in the best possible condition. At the same time, dancers must reach and maintain a creative and artistic edge that enables them to touch the audience night after night.

Dancer and experimentalist choreographer Murray Louis put it eloquently when he said, "Dancers work and live from the inside. They are almost always in pain, physically and mentally. The responsibility of keeping in shape is never ending and crushing. They can never let down. The intensity of behavior, which laymen find trying, is, for the dancer, essential. They drive themselves constantly, producing a glow that lights not only themselves, but audience after audience." There is a physical and mental vulnerability involved in dance, as dancers not only expose their bodies but their very souls.

Moreover, people entering into a career in dance know that from a very early age that they have to make sacrifices. Young dancers must forego many of the things their peers find so interesting; indeed, they must often give up friendships in order to maintain the discipline of their craft. As young adults, dancers in major companies find themselves touring from town to town and country to country, in the process leaving behind important personal relationships, connections with families, and a settled home life. Mikhail Baryshnikov, whose name is synonymous with dance today, put it this way: "Nobody is born to be a dancer. To be a dancer you must want it more than anything. You don't know in the beginning whether you will succeed. And then you don't know until later whether you will be injured and must stop. But you must live a disciplined life. The desire to be a dancer is the discipline of a career, and your work is the language of that discipline." Choreographer George Balanchine was even more blunt in saying, "First comes the sweat then comes the beauty."

Why do dancers endure the pain, the agony, and the hard work that is required of them? Basically, it's a matter of passion, commitment, and dedication. For the best dancers that sense of dedication is intense, an all-consuming fire blazing inside and manifest externally as a willingness to do whatever is necessary to be the best they can be. Twyla Tharp, who has worked with the great ballet companies as well as choreographed for film, stage, and television, spoke of the "will" that is required to succeed in the world of dance: "I also had a will that let me eliminate everything that stood in the way of my becoming the best dancer I could be. By a gradual process . . . I had invested every bit of my dreams, my hopes, my energies in defining myself as a dancer."

There are many artists who don't have that dedication and they are limited in what they can do. In our interview, internationally known jazz trombonist Vincent Nilsson remarked, "Very often I have students who want to be able to play, but they are not prepared to do the work. They have quite good talent but don't do the work. It's quite sad." He then added ironically, "Of course, it's a talent to be able to do the work too." Unfortunately, not all artists have that talent for practice and hard work.

But for those who are willing to make the commitment and engage in the hours, days, months, and years that are required to be the best, the joy of the performance is quite special. In working on this project, we have been struck by the contrast between the hard work of the dancer's occupation and the moments of glorious expression on stage. That irony, of course, was what inspired the French impressionist painter Edgar Degas as he painted the ballerina. Rarely did he capture the actual performance, preferring instead to capture the drudgery of the dancer's day-to-day life. Yet flowing from that drudgery was the ultimate magic of the performance. Past the hard work, the dance ultimately brings a special joy. In our interview, David Parsons captured the irony of the dancer's life in this way: "Some days it's just like pulling teeth. You've got a creak or an injury. You've got a cold. You've been on a plane. Then there's days where you are just on automatic and you're in a mode that is just bliss. You feel the energy going out. And the greatest thing is that you don't even know what it is. But you feel it."

Many of the dancers and choreographers we interviewed talked about the passion that they had for dance or the passion that they wished to express through their dancing or choreography. Nowhere was that sense of passion more clearly expressed than in a fascinating conversation we had with Tamara Nijinsky and Kinga Gaspers, the daughter and granddaughter of the legendary Russian dancer Vaslav Nijinsky. Nijinsky, called the greatest dancer of the twentieth century, "The God of the Dance," was known worldwide for his technical precision, his artistic virtuosity, and his vivid dramatic portrayals. But at the height of his career, he began to experience a series of psychological problems that led him in and out of mental hospitals through the remainder of his life. At the edge of his madness, Nijinsky wrote an incredible semi-biographical/semi-philosophical tract titled "The Diary of Vaslav Nijinsky," which was the subject of a recent and highly acclaimed documentary film.

Tamara Nijinsky and Kinga Gaspers described Nijinsky as someone completely driven by a love of his fellow human beings, a love of peace, and the hope that he could express that love through his dancing and choreography. "His art was his life. He didn't separate. He was a dancer, an artist twenty-four hours a day. That was the air he breathed, and when he became ill a part of his illness was that he couldn't work, he couldn't create." Nijinsky had a vision of a peaceful world where people would love and understand one another, and he wanted to help create this world through his gift, his art. He wrote in his diary, "My madness is my love for mankind." He also wrote, "You will understand me when you see me dance."

Nijinsky's effect on all those with whom he came into contact was compelling. Those who saw him dance still comment on seeing something incredible. Even many who knew him only through the diary speak of the impact Nijinsky has had on them. His granddaughter remarked, "When he came into the room, there was an aura, a peace, a serenity. He brought some kind of calm into the room." His passion was his artistry, his creativity, and his dancing. But it was his passion as much as his artistry, his creativity, or his dancing that comes through in one's learning about Nijinsky. While other artists may not so clearly reveal their passion as did Nijinsky, that passion is what causes dancers to endure the hard work, the pain, and the sacrifice, and to express themselves in ways that audiences find enchanting and energizing.

Like dancers, leaders work extremely hard and must be firmly committed to, even passionate about, what they are doing. While we think that's true for leaders at all levels, hard work especially characterizes leadership at the highest levels. The hours are long, the levels of stress often extreme, and the pressures to produce are extraordinary. Lattie Coor put it this way: "I would never presume that I have dedicated the whole of my professional life the way a dancer does. But a university presidency is a way of life; it's not a job, it's undertaking a venture. You live it day and night. You need to organize private space in your life; indeed, if you don't, you won't be a good leader. But you organize your private space within that life rather than the other way around."

The leader's role is consuming in many ways—time-consuming, life-consuming. In order to commit to the hard work of leadership, leaders need to be clear about what they are doing. William Jacobs, president of the Western Institutional Review Board, stated what might seem obvious, but many fail to grasp: "If you are going to be a leader, you have to have a reason to be a leader—an agenda, a vision, a reason for being." For some it will be the substance of the work. When we asked City Manager Jan Perkins about what motivates her to spend so many long and often difficult hours on the job, she replied that it was her deep commitment to democratic local government and the feeling that she could make a difference. For others, the passion will reside in chasing a dream. But the pursuit of a dream is itself not easy, especially because other people may not share the dream or even believe that it's attainable. Consequently, many may discourage the dream, making it even more difficult to attain.

Larry Newman, who invented, built, and made a million dollars selling the ultra-light airplane, shared with us his experience in fighting off what he called "the dream stealers": "You have a dream and everybody wants to steal it away from you. They try to take it away from you by saying things like, 'Why are you doing that? It's silly.' But they just don't get it. If more people just said, 'I'm not going to listen to anybody. I'm just going to succeed,' we could do wonderful things." Success is sometimes a matter of tenacity, clinging to the dream when everyone around you is saying it will never work. Imagine how many people might say that to you if you told them you were going to make some money by putting a motor on a hang glider. Yet that's exactly what Larry Newman did—and it worked.

Doing something you enjoy, believing in what you are doing, and being passionate about it is as important to leaders as to dancers. It's also contagious. Just as Vaslav Nijinsky's passion for his art seemed to affect those he came in contact with, the passion, the commitment, the energy, and the enthusiasm a leader shows for his or her work will be felt by others and may cause them to enlist in the cause. An element of artistic leadership is not only to have passion for one's work as a self-motivating force, though that is clearly important. The leader's passion is also something others see and feel. It creates an emotional resonance and draws them to the leader. The energy and enthusiasm a leader shows can itself be an energizing force, and that's what leadership is all about, whether you are talking about a family, a work group, or a large organization.

Confidence and Humility

Dancers and leaders both engage in very public actions. Dancers appear on stage before audiences of thousands, where every little mistake can be seen and remembered. Leaders, while less often appearing in such formal settings as an auditorium, are "on" all the time with people listening to every syllable and observing every little body movement as a sign of something significant. For most people, situations like these are invitations to stress, nervousness, and possible disaster. There are, of course, "tricks" to combat "stage fright," whether on stage or in a conference room. For example, meditation or breathing exercises may help with nervousness and fatigue. But there is a deeper sense in which dancers and leaders need to establish a foundation upon which their skills can be exercised. Both need to develop a strong sense of confidence in themselves and in others with whom they work.

While leaders rarely talk about the importance of confidence, dancers have long discussed this topic and indeed a part of their training has to do with building confidence. Choreographer Doris Humphrey, for example, identified the problem this way: "The dancer with conviction has power; many a dance of poor quality has been 'put across' just by the superb belief of the performer in the work. . . . If you believe in yourself, everybody else probably will, too." Similarly, Cem Catbas of the Ballet Academy of Baltimore told us, "Before you go on stage, you have to think you are the greatest, because only then will the audience believe that you are."

Clearly, dancers who have a lot of confidence in themselves and their partners will be more relaxed during the performance, while those who don't will likely become more anxious—and that will in turn limit their performance even further. This is not to say, however, that only dancers who have limited skills are affected by nervousness and can be affected by it in their performance. Even dancers who are technically very strong and capable but don't believe in themselves will have problems.

How do dancers build confidence? First, and obviously, the better prepared you are the less nervous you will be, whereas if your technique or understanding is shaky, you will be more nervous. Second, just as we spoke earlier about thinking too much during the performance, overanalyzing your own psychological condition is not especially helpful either. By maintaining a strong focus on the performance, you won't be tempted to wonder whether people can see how nervous you are, something that will only make you more nervous. Third, dance educators point out that the best dancers carry themselves differently from those who are less gifted, something they attribute to self-confidence. By carrying themselves differently dancers may be able to influence their level of self-confidence. "Dancers can influence how they think and feel by how they carry themselves." Fourth, as dancers mature, some argue, they think less about themselves and what the audience thinks of them and more about the performance and the artistry they can bring to it. The mime Robert Shields told us, "When you are a young performer, you're thinking about the audience. Now when I perform it's special, because I'm finally out of the way."

With respect to what others can do to help build one's confidence, we heard similar comments from both artistic directors in major dance companies and coaches in major college sports about what a rehearsal director or coach can do to help build self-confidence. Roy Kaiser of the Pennsylvania Ballet commented on the balance that's necessary in building confidence: "I want to bring the best out of each individual dancer—and they are all different. For some it's building confidence, for some it's restraining confidence. Overconfidence is dangerous, overconfidence doesn't read well. There's just a zone—you need just enough to allow yourself to perform at your best." Similarly, basketball coach Ernie Kent of Oregon talked about his positive approach to building confidence: "I want to give you all the confidence I can give you. I'm going to tell you what you *can* do. I'm not going to stop you by putting limits on you, saying you can't do something. I'm going to give you the confidence, the platform to grow from."

Obviously, the lessons described here can be helpful to leaders as well and indeed many of the leaders we talked with made similar points, both about how to build your own confidence and how to build the confidence of others. University president Dave Frohnmayer drew a parallel between the role of the leader and that of a conductor (one of his avocations): "The conductor's job is to make the ensemble as rich as possible. You can exercise an enormous amount of leadership just through what you convey. That depends in significant part on the confidence that you project (and that can be mastered). It is important that you convey that confidence or the orchestra won't have any reason to follow your gestures. The conductor's role is to keep the tributaries from overflowing the banks, so that they all contribute to the ultimate grand flow of the river."

For the leader as for the dancer, it is important that confidence not turn into overconfidence. Especially for the leader, it's important that confidence be balanced with a sense of humility and respect for others. On the one hand, or perhaps for some people, leadership can be a very humbling experience. Jeanette Harrison, chief learning officer of Intel, described to us her response to being thrust into a position where people expected her to lead: "No matter how many books you read, no matter how many discussions you have, when you are standing in front of a group of a hundred or two hundred people and you are responsible for energizing those people, eliminating the roadblocks they may find, enabling them to do great things—that is a very humbling experience."

The pressure of such expectations can help to maintain a sense of humility, but there are pressures in the other direction as well. Tom Downs, Amtrak chief executive, who was earlier city administrator of Washington, D.C, spoke of the temptation for leaders to believe their own press and to become deluded into thinking it's all about them. In his view, we live in an age of "celebrity," so that leaders sometimes lack balance and perspective. The sense of celebrity that accompanies people in high positions is such that others around them start "kissing up," to the point that the leader starts to believe what they are saying. "It's a very seductive thing because you think you are the webmaster, the master of the universe. The word 'hubris' comes from the Greek, a combination of aspiration and tragedy. It has the seeds of its own destruction. No matter what the size of your organization, it can happen to you." The antidote, according to Downs, is to rediscover the value of humility and to maintain a healthy and unambiguous respect for others.

General Ron Fogleman made the same point, though connecting the issue of humility to that of integrity: "The essence of leadership is integrity. You need to be focused on the mission and your people and not yourself. The leader should be selfless in every dimension of the word." Over the years, Fogleman argued, it is important to develop a sense of integrity that guides your decisions, so that it's not just your personal preference at the moment. "In the course of growing up, you develop an inner moral and professional compass. Based on your professional expertise and the moral dimension to the decision that has to be made, there comes a point where the situation calls for a decision. You look at the facts you have available, you make a decision, and you press on. It's the professional expertise and the moral compass that allows you to do that."

Finally, a part of appropriate humility is to recognize that you don't know everything. Indeed, at least one leader we talked with considered humility to be a foundation for leadership, maybe even a defining distinction between managers and leaders. Bob Johnson of Honeywell Aerospace commented, "I think to be a good leader you start with not knowing. When you are the chief scientist or the chief financial person, you got there by being the best and knowing it all. To be a leader you have to give it all up. Leadership is about not already knowing and being able to listen." In other words, being humble and listening is not only the right thing to do, it works.

The Inner Resources

If you watch candidates for high public office campaigning, whatever you think of their politics, you can't help but be impressed by their energy, their enthusiasm, and simply their stamina, their physical ability to keep going day after day. The same is true of top-level executives in business, in universities, in the military, and in the world of sports. Phil Tyson was just such a person. Phil had held a number of high-level positions before taking over a struggling high-tech firm in California, so he must have known what he was getting into. But the zest and dedication with which he undertook his new responsibilities still surprised many. Not only were there company meetings from early in the morning until sometimes late into the evening, Phil also made a commitment to the community and became engaged in activities ranging from reviewing the state's economic development policy to encouraging greater support for the arts.

People marveled at the physical demands on Phil, but in a private conversation with a friend he confessed that the mental part of the game was much more difficult. "I do make time for exercise and I practice a number of different stress management techniques, though people rarely see those parts of my day. And frankly I enjoy what I'm doing so much, I actually think it's healthy for me. So the physical part is not as hard as people think." But, he continued, the real challenges are mental. They have to do with knowing myself, staying in touch with my own values, and simply being true to myself. "There are many things that can distract you—money, celebrity, and attention among them. But you have to maintain a balance, a connection to what's really important in your life. For me to change our company means that I have to change myself. I have to come to fully and unequivocally accept the new direction that we're going. If I don't believe in what we're doing, no one else will." For the best leaders, maintaining their own integrity, in every sense of the word, is the hardest but most important part of leading.

Making Meaning

As we have already seen, the leader is very much engaged in "making meaning." The leader is interested in constructing new lenses through which people can see the future and see one another moving into that future together with a sense of energy and flow. Leadership is the capacity to interpret reality in ways that really help others understand better what might be possible. It's about establishing a context. In this sense, leadership is not just about coming up with good ideas or solving problems, either with respect to the substance of the group's work or the process by which things get done. Certainly those contributions by the leader are valued and people resonate with the leader's confident capacity to develop ingenious ways around disputes or obstacles that seem ready to slow the group's progress.

But in making meaning, leaders are performing a far more difficult task. People need meaning perhaps more than anything else. They need to know that what they are doing makes sense, that it has some longer-term value. Making meaning, therefore, has to do with both providing a context for human action and framing the significance of the group's work. In our view, these dual aspects of the leader's making meaning for or on behalf of a group can be addressed through some of the skills we discussed in connection with our consideration of empathetic listening and evocative speaking. But at an even deeper level the process of making meaning is fully rooted in the leader's psyche, perhaps even the leader's soul. It is something that draws on some of the leader's most vital and precious inner resources and should be framed in that fashion.

Again, the lessons from the world of dance are fascinating. A dance, of course, is typically not intended just for entertainment, but rather seeks to convey feelings, emotions, impressions, meanings. A dance seeks to "touch the viewer, to communicate a sense, vision, idea, style, texture, or quality. It has an attitude about it, an aura of uniqueness, a selfhood." We would say the leader's efforts to make meaning are similarly oriented. The leader seeks to express, in words, in approach, in style, in movement, in whatever way possible, a vision of the future, again not necessarily one that the leader alone has divined but one that the leader has constructed from the contributions of many others. The leader provides clues, impressions, symbols, metaphors, interpretations as to the emotional engagement to which others might commit themselves in order to make a better future. And, in doing so, the leader affects the values that will shape a group's future.

As we said, some of the leader's messages relate to the *context*—how things are situated and how they fit together. In order for any one element in a system to perform at its best, it must fit with its context. Similarly, for individuals to perform at their best, they must have a comprehension of the fundamental ideas that define the framework within which they operate—what one writer called, "an organic unity of feeling" that can bring "coherence and flow to what would otherwise be only a loosely related collection of parts." While there may be no obvious systemic unity among members of a group or organization, the leader can provide an "organic unity of feeling" that can bring unity and flow to the group. In fact, only through providing a context for action that makes sense will the leader be able to shape the flow of energy that his or her leadership releases.

Another part of making meaning has to do with establishing the *significance* of what is being undertaken. In an age that has been described as fragmented and chaotic, people especially need a sense of meaning and significance in their lives. They want to know that what they are doing will make a difference, that it will extend beyond the immediate moment and impact the future, hopefully in some positive way. For this reason, leaders, like other artists, play an important role in identifying and orienting people toward the most important issues in a particular time and place. They give form to what is especially meaningful and significant in the lives of the people with whom they interact. Judy Mohraz of the Piper Foundation talked with us about some of the concerns that leaders today must attend to. They include "a profoundly personal understanding of what people want to do with their lives; why we're here on this earth; and how do you help someone find meaning, find personal and professional growth, and find connectedness with the larger."

There is an awesome responsibility associated with the leader's role as an artist, because the artist must not only engage the audience, but also confront the "spirit" of the age in which he or she lives. Artists must connect with the specific audience present on any given night, but they must also work from the experience of their culture and their time (and how it fits with those before and after). The leader is involved in something like a "conversation," a dialogue with people immediately present but also with many far away in both space and time, those whose thoughts and ideas have shaped the current situation and those whose actions will shape the future.

Again, Judy Mohraz spoke eloquently about the way that leaders engage the time, the age in which they live and work. She first noted that art often takes long-standing symbols or traditions and reinterprets them for the current time and place. While there may be continuity, there may also be a major break with the past, a new way of seeing and interpreting reality. "And that's often what a leader is doing. In some instances taking something long-established and trying to reinterpret it in a new and more dynamic and relevant way, and in other instances simply breaking with the known and striking out in a very new and innovative way. Institutions may require one kind of leader at one point and another kind of leader at another." (That probably explains why you have artists or leaders that are ahead of their time.)

But through the engagement of leaders with their time and their surroundings, through the dialogue we mentioned before, there must emerge a complete clarity of intent; the leader must know what the game is all about. That is not to say that the leader must or ever will know the outcome of the game in advance. But the leader must know what the game is. The leader must develop a perspective, an intent, and an articulated viewpoint that is at once creative, carefully constructed, challenging, and ultimately compelling. That's not easy work, and in the process the leader can get pulled in many different directions. Some of it can get pretty risky, both for the group or organization and for the leader personally. Dancer and choreographer Daniel Nagrin wrote, "Traversing the tightrope of art requires a balance between infinite care and reckless abandon." Certainly the same is true of leadership, and that task is made considerably easier if the leader is firmly grounded. Dance and choreographer Charles Weidman expressed it nicely when he said, "The artist must not run away from himself, his 'center of being.' He is the bearer of a message, and it is his responsibility to tell it—in whatever medium it may be—intelligibly, forcefully and with his utmost artistic ability. He may sometimes fail in the delivery of this message, but he must never fail in his purpose."

Effecting Change

We are familiar with all the dichotomies that mark modern life—theory and practice, subject and object, fantasy and reality, to mention just a few. What is interesting is that dance and leadership both transcend these distinctions. Art engages these various conflicts as tensions to be resolved. For example, using the tension between fantasy and reality as his example, dance educator John Wilson told us that art is concerned on the one hand with the things the artist would like to perpetuate and on the other with those things the artist would like to transcend: "The purpose of art is to generate and maintain conflicts between the world as we find it to be and the world of imagination." That, of course, is precisely the world of leadership as well.

Leadership involves change, indeed, leadership is crucially and uniquely situated just at the moment of change, right at the crossroads we encounter as we move from the past through the present and into the future. The special contribution of leadership is to help groups and organizations resolve questions about the future. But, of course, doing so is anything but simple. While the act of leading doesn't allow such a rational explanation as it occurs, we might say that leadership involves helping the group work through an assessment of its history, its future, and even what we might call the history of the future, that is, what the future will look like in retrospect days or months or years from now. It involves integrating and articulating the path or direction that the group or organization chooses. And it involves stimulating or triggering the release of energy that most characterizes successful group action and helping to guide the flow of energy that results as the group moves forward. As we have said before, leadership energizes and energy brings about change.

Again, the process of change is the dynamic that moves us beyond ordinary dichotomies of life. Change involves action, and action, for example, can never involve pure theory or pure practice alone. Speaking of the world of dance, Randy Martin, professor of art and public policy at New York University, describes that condition in this way: "Dance generates a sense of being in the midst of a crisis, a break, a rupture, even a loss and a prospect at the same time; thus while dancing may appear to be a series of stops and starts, for the dancer, next steps are already in motion, already passing from one (im)balance to another." Martin's phrasing brings to mind a description of Doris Humphrey's approach to dance: "All movement can be considered to be a series of falls and recoveries; that is, a deliberate unbalance in order to progress, and a restoration of equilibrium for self-protection. The nearer the state of unbalance approaches the dangerous the more exciting it becomes to watch, and the more pleasurable the recovery. This danger zone, which life tends to avoid as much as possible, is the zone in which the dance largely has its existence."

But leaders also inhabit this zone, working in a time and space that others hesitate to enter, always flirting with the tension between gain and loss, pleasure and pain, the present and the future, and always working with the energy available to them. The forces that are at play in the act of leading are powerful indeed and require the utmost strength and character on the part of the leader to merely withstand the vicissitudes of change, much less to help the world move in a positive direction. Leaders must have an inner strength and bearing that will provide a stable foundation for their actions as well as a strong sense of morality or integrity that will provide support as they assume the responsibility that ultimately will be placed at their doorstep.

The expectations of space and time and energy that we discussed earlier bear heavily on the leader. Leadership occurs in the moment, often in a very passing moment, yet in its impact leadership far exceeds that moment, often affecting worlds far different in space and time through the energy it disposes. Change involves loss and pain, yet we expect leaders to provide the sense of context and significance that will give us faith to endure that pain and loss in the hopes of a better future. The world of the leader is in some ways quite a lonely world, a world in which the leader must work through his or her own inner demons (and perhaps call on special angels) on the way to resolving an artistic approach to change and to the future.

Though he was writing about the artist, we think that the philosopher Walter Sorell expressed the leader's predicament extremely well:

> The artist creates out of the world that has made him in order to remake it according to the image of his inner world. His struggle to give this image meaning and form is basically a struggle with himself. It goes without saying that he is tortured by a compulsive feeling to express himself through his artistic medium. He is cursed with a heightened sensitivity and awareness to do so. He feels hurled into a lifelong struggle, using and discarding the heritage of yesterday, finding the true expression of today, which, at the same time, envisions the face and shape of another tomorrow. In other words, no artist can deny his past, and even in rebelling against it he pays his negating respects to it. He must realize that yesterday was a living today as much as he must be aware of the fact that there will be no artistic tomorrow if his today is not burningly alive.

We need not dwell here on the "metaphysics" of change or the way in which the leader confronts his or her angel, muse, or what some have called the "duende." But it is important to recognize that leadership, the act of leading, is not just about methods or techniques or procedures by which change can be brought about. That treatment of leadership, which is, we think, all too familiar, denies the very personal and deep-seated struggles that leaders endure as they practice their calling, whether in the most mundane settings or those involving matters of paramount economic or political importance. Leadership is far more deeply rooted in the human psyche than we tend to acknowledge. We think that is because the world has focused excessively on the science of leadership, a topic that is amenable to the rational use of technique, and has vastly underestimated the art of leadership, which clearly is not. Recognizing the artistic dimension of leadership, however, compels us to acknowledge and give further thought to the inner resources required by the leader.

Integrity and Authenticity

It may seem odd to use the term *morality* in relation to art. After all, artists seek to evoke emotion, but sometimes those emotions are disgust, revulsion, and rage. Is this moral? While there is no simple answer to that question, the question itself is still vitally important. What is important for the purposes here is that because art and leadership seek to touch us in a way that involves our values and emotions, they necessarily involve questions of morality. Art, like leadership, is to a great extent in the eyes of the beholder. If we experience art that we consider to be wrong or immoral, and inconsistent with our values, we are likely to walk away. If the work seems phony, insincere, and inauthentic, we are likely to become closed to the message the artist may be trying to convey. Artists feel strongly that they must be true to their art and authentic in their bodies, and they accept that, ultimately, their art will be experienced and judged by others.

Leaders confront these same kinds of tensions. They certainly push the envelope; they challenge us to think, feel, and do things that may go beyond our comfort level. But they also recognize that if they cannot be true to both themselves and the larger purposes they serve, if they are perceived as lacking integrity and moral grounding, if they do not authentically connect with the people around them, others simply will not follow. This moral grounding is based on a number of things: knowledge of themselves and their own values, the values and aspirations of those they lead and serve, and a purpose larger than themselves that they and the people that they work with can believe and trust is valuable, good, and worthy of giving the best of themselves.

So we return to the idea we mentioned early on, that leadership is a moral venture, based on integrity, authenticity, and, at the risk of sounding trite, a deep-seated desire to do the right thing. While some leadership experts would argue that anyone who achieves significant change is a leader, we firmly reject this idea. Leadership can and should and must be more than that. Ultimately, what we all yearn for, and increasingly need, are leaders who stand for something that we can believe in and feel good about. We want leaders with integrity and moral grounding whom we can trust to be what they claim and to do the right thing. We need and want leaders to tap what is best in us and energize us to work with creativity and joy.

Reprise

In our view, the leader must possess certain skills in order to lead, or, to put it differently, for others to perceive him or her as a leader. But those skills are embedded in a set of personal disciplines and inner resources. The skills of the leader are important, but they are not employed randomly. Instead, they are given shape and direction through the disciplines that leaders employ, disciplines such as focus and concentration, hard work, passion, and a blend of confidence and humility. Moreover, the leader's skills are only capable of use in ways that are authentically consistent with the leader's view of the world, the values the leader holds, and the leader's understanding of how change is brought about. These inner resources, authentically held and deeply valued, go to the very basis of the leader's ability to help shape human energy in a positive direction. We like performance artist Elizabeth Keen's statement about choreography: "If someone choreographs a dance worth its salt, the quantity of good rises in the world." We believe that if someone engages in an act of leadership worth its salt, in whatever setting, at whatever level, the quantity of good in the world also rises.

7

Learning the Art of Leadership

"How do I learn to be a leader?" someone asked. "By reading textbooks? By studying the lives of great leaders? By watching leaders in action?"

"How would you learn to dance?" came the response. "By reading textbooks? By studying the lives of great dancers? By watching dancers in action?"

"No, of course not. That would barely be a beginning."

"You're right. You only learn to dance by dancing. And you only learn to lead by leading."

We have said that there are not only parallels between art and leadership, but that there are certain key elements of leadership that are fully artistic in nature. These essential features of the art of leading are common to leadership at all levels of society, whether in families, small groups, large organizations, or societies, and in all sectors, whether public, private, nonprofit, the military, education, or sports. There are certain things that people do and certain personal qualities they exhibit that "connect" with others by creating an emotional bond between the leader and the follower that people experience as social energy. As this energy is given shape and direction through the interactions of members of the group or organization, we can say that the group has been energized or, to put it differently, an act of leadership has occurred. The act of leading results in a flow of human energy in a particular direction and at a particular speed and tempo.

Among the ways in which leaders "connect" with others, most have the capacity to comprehend and in subtle ways alter the rhythms and tempos at which groups and organizations move, a part of which occurs through the leader's superior sense of timing, knowing when it is just the right time for the group to act. In addition, leaders, more than others, tend to communicate in images, symbols, and metaphors that touch the human emotions. Specifically, leaders are more likely to engage in empathetic listening and evocative speaking, both of which contribute to their special connection with others, a connection that is the basis for leadership. Leaders also establish a sense of connection through their often uncanny ability to engage in improvised speech, which, when it is accomplished with creativity and spontaneity, touches the emotions in a way that builds the confidence of group members in the leader. Finally, in addition to these skills associated with the act of leading, leaders rely on certain inner disciplines and inner resources. These are the qualities that provide a foundation for their creative contribution to making meaning in society and help them bring about effective and responsible change.

We don't claim that these are the only ways that leaders lead. Sometimes people who simply have good ideas are seen as leaders. Sometimes those who know the work inside and out are considered leaders. Sometimes those with the most sophisticated intellectual understanding of those problems facing the group or organization are seen as leaders. In these cases, however, leaders depend more on their rational and technical expertise and a corresponding form of communication. While some may lead in this way, effective leaders more often lead through building the kinds of emotional connection we have described here. So is leadership an art or a science? In most situations, we suspect that leadership is typically a combination of science and art. But, as those with experience in the real world consistently say, it is clear that the artistic dimension of leadership is both the most often practiced and the least understood.

By looking at the world of art, music, and especially dance, we have been able to identify certain key elements of the art of leadership. There are certain things that leaders do that cause others to follow. Among these, two are most important: *Leaders connect with us emotionally, in a way that energizes us and moves us to act. And leaders provide the assurance that we need to pursue important values.* These are the central elements of the art of leadership and the keys to understanding and eventually developing greater artistry as a leader.

These acts of leadership, these behaviors that people take as acts of leading, are not by any means new. Indeed, people have engaged in these kinds of actions for decades, even centuries. But recently leadership studies have focused more on the science of leadership and these elements have become less valued. In contrast, a new understanding of the artistic dimensions of leadership such as we have developed here not only provides a language for understanding and giving voice to these less-recognized but extremely important aspects of leadership, it also permits leaders far more breadth and flexibility in their actions.

We have suggested that there are certain kinds of actions and certain inner qualities that people respond to by becoming energized. For some, these acts of leading are natural. These are the people we call "born" leaders. Still others try to improve their capacity for leadership through study, learning, and practice. They may seek out mentors, they may be especially attentive to what the most effective leaders do, and they may read articles and books on leadership. But mostly for this group, developing leadership skills is more the result of experience and self-reflection. They note when people follow and when they don't. Either intellectually or just subconsciously, these aspiring leaders begin to emphasize those things that work and eliminate those that don't.

Unfortunately, much of what passes for leadership development today misses some of these important ideas. Obviously, you don't learn how to paint just by visiting museums, galleries, and exhibitions. You don't learn how to play music merely by going to clubs, concerts, or listening to the best CDs. And you don't learn dance just by going to the ballet every week. Though you may pick up a few tips along the way, something else is necessary in order for the artist to learn his or her craft. That something is experience and practice, combined with regular and detailed feedback and self-reflection.

Too often, in our view, those who want to learn to lead are told to watch successful leaders, either historical leaders or just those in the workplace, to note the traits and characteristics that seem to make them successful, then to try to reproduce the behaviors that they engage in. To support that approach to leadership development, various scholars, especially management theorists, have tried to identify, through scientific studies, those traits and characteristics that potential followers find most appealing and those behaviors leaders can engage in that are consistent with those expectations. For example, studies find that people want their leaders to be credible. So the recommendation to the potential leader is, "Be credible"—an admonition that sounds good in theory but is extremely difficult to put into practice. Moreover, credibility is difficult to assess in one's own behavior: how do you know when you are perceived as credible and when you are not?

We noted earlier that artistic aspects of leadership like improvisation and timing are easy to recognize in the work of leaders, but are rarely addressed in the literature on leadership. Isn't it curious that while leaders always say, "Timing is everything," there is almost no mention of timing in the literature on management and leadership. (That's probably because that literature addresses the science of management and leadership, rather than the art.) Art, music, and dance, on the other hand, clearly understand the importance of improvisation and timing. They are not only considered legitimate topics for discussion and study, they are considered essential.

Even more important, over the years, those in the arts have developed clear educational strategies for teaching and learning these skills. There are, in fact, art institutes, schools of music, and dance studios all over the world that are premised on the fact that one's art can be developed and improved over time. Art generally, and, we would say, the art of leadership, may require some basic skills, and admittedly, some people seem to be born with a certain genius for these skills. But artists all agree that whatever the level of innate talent and ability, one's art can be advanced, cultivated, and refined through a combination of practice, instruction, and experience. In this chapter, we will examine the strategy for learning that is basic to the arts and some of the lessons that we can draw from arts education for leadership education.

The Studio Experience

What is most obvious about arts education, what differentiates it most easily from typical classroom instruction, is the studio experience. Painters and sculptures first learn their craft in the studio; musicians work together in rehearsals and labs; and dancers, even professional dancers, take daily "classes" in the studio, typically equipped with a barre and a mirror on one wall. As a physical setting for learning, the studio appears quite different from other types of classrooms, most of which are still marked by rows of desks and chairs.

What is probably most important for our purposes is not the physical setting, but the approaches to learning that the studio implies and indeed encourages. Learning skill-based disciplines is simply different from learning math or biology. As we noted above, traditional approaches to leadership development remain primarily cognitive, that is, students are asked to learn about leadership traits and characteristics, then examine those through the experiences or biographies of well-known leaders. We suggest that the most effective leadership education has to involve students in learning both at the cognitive level *and* at the interpersonal and personal level.

Think about the way you acquire any set of skills, whether in art, music, painting, dance, golf, tennis, or whatever. First you can gain cognitive information about the skill. For example, if you want to improve your golf game, you can read books by Jack Nicklaus, David Leadbetter, or Tiger Woods. From these books you will acquire an intellectual understanding of the game. But just learning that much doesn't necessarily improve your game. Instead, you have to move to a second level; you have to practice the skills over and over until you acquire the physical skill to execute the movement correctly. You have to practice, practice, practice. You have to spend hours and hours on the practice range until your shots go where you want them to. Even then, when you get out on the course under conditions that are a little more complex and uncertain, even stressful, you may not perform as well as you did when you were on the practice range. In golf, but also in other sports, as well as in art, music, and dance, what you need is a kind of psychological "grounding" that enables you to do successfully what you know to be correct and what you have practiced successfully many times before.

The same sequence of learning is important in the development of leaders as well. You can learn about leadership from the many books on leadership, even this one. But even if you "know" the skills that are needed, you are going to have to practice those skills over and over. For most leaders, this practice is called *experience* and involves basically a trial-and-error approach in which you try one thing and if it doesn't work you try something else. But practice can occur in a more specific and well-constructed fashion, incorporating extensive feedback and coaching. Still, there is one further step that must be taken, and that is for the potential leaders to acquire the moral and psychological grounding that will enable them to do what they know to be right and what they have done correctly time after time. This moral and psychological grounding, which we have previously referred to in terms of the leader's inner resources, is clearly related to the leader's maturity, self-esteem, and authenticity. It is largely a product of self-reflection and self-critique.

Let's examine the studio experience as a setting for and an approach to learning. First, the studio is a place not primarily used for didactic instruction but for practice and creative experimentation. Second, the studio setting brings the instructor and students together in a collaborative relationship in which all are involved in generating ideas, executing those ideas, and providing feedback to each other. Third, the studio encourages, and in fact demands, a considerable amount of individual self-reflection. Consider the implications of each of these features.

First, the studio encourages practice and creative experimentation. It is not designed for instruction by the "teacher," and is different from a lecture hall in this sense. The studio is not intended as a place in which to communicate textbook information, but as one in which to develop skills. In the studio, students learn from their actual experiences, including their sharing of material developed in the studio and material developed outside and then brought into the studio. It is a place in which the skills that the group is exploring in any particular session are tried out, corrected, and practiced again. Especially in advanced work, there is rarely a right or wrong answer, a right or wrong way to do something. Rather, students are encouraged to come up with new approaches, new interpretations, and to experiment with new ways of doing things.

The studio encourages students not to practice one right way of doing something but to create new ways of approaching familiar material. As dance instructor Claudia Murphey put it, "If plan A doesn't work, try something else. Allow yourself multiple solutions to a problem. If there's a roadblock, try to be creative and find a way around that roadblock. We want to always feel that we're moving forward, not spinning." The musician, painter, or dancer may try something that simply doesn't work, but in the studio setting they have the opportunity to come up with something else and try again. Obviously, this approach is one that stimulates students to learn creative problem solving.

Second, the studio creates a collaborative relationship among all involved. We asked Andre Lewis, artistic director of the Royal Winnipeg Ballet, what was different about the studio as a setting for learning. "There's much more interactivity, I think, between the people, between the ideas that people may have. At a desk you are essentially on your own. We've always done our art in a studio, working out things together. That develops a sense of camaraderie and openness, and usually brings energy out of people." Lewis's ideas were echoed by David Miller of the award-winning architectural firm the Miller/Hull Partnership in speaking about architectural education: "A lot of collaboration occurs because you are working in the same room. In the room together, there are multiple ideas that you can then take forward and get it built." The studio experience is typically a highly interactive, participatory, and involving experience for students, one in which a lot of give-and-take occurs.

In a class in choreography, for example, a student or a small group might be given an "improv," an idea around which to create a movement sequence. The individual or group then performs the "dance" they have choreographed. The instructor and the other students then consider ways in which the idea might be expressed differently. After some discussion, the individual or group might rework their "improv" and present it again. And the cycle continues. The intent is for students to build on the ideas of others, not to block each other's ideas. (There is far less competition in the studio than is built into certain classrooms—for example, the law school lecture room.) The studio atmosphere is typically one of cooperation and encouragement rather than competition. It provides a chance for students to do the work, to reflect upon what they have done, and to talk about what it means and what alternative approaches there might be.

Third, the studio encourages self-reflection. Any particular student, especially in advanced classes, is likely to receive only one or two direct comments an hour from the instructor. Students are encouraged, however, to learn from the instructor's comments to other students as well as those directed to them personally. Moreover, each person must engage in a significant amount of self-reflection to translate the comments and conversations around them into lessons that apply to their own work. Some ideas will be more relevant to one person than another. It is largely up to the student to sort out the information that is being passed about and incorporate in their own work that which seems most helpful. Active self-reflection not only improves the dancer's specific skills, but also supports a creative approach to their work and indeed their lives in general.

Roger Bedard, theater instructor, described the way in which the studio approach contributes to the student's self-understanding: "You help these people find out where their strengths and weaknesses are, as an artist, and challenge them to address them, given the space and the confidence to work." In the studio, students are trained to find their own sense of expression, whether a brush stroke, a musical phrasing, or an approach to movement. However, it's important to note that some students are not completely ready for such self-revelation and that the studio must create a safe haven for learning: "You have to put them in a place where it's safe enough for them to explore who they are. And that is something that is really revolutionary for many, a huge identity crisis," says Bedard.

Lessons from Learning the Arts

Roughly related to the three aspects of the studio experience are three aspects of learning art that we heard described by artists, all of which have interesting implications for leadership development. The first has to do with experimentation and the contingent nature of the work. Again, artists, unlike most scientists, are not looking for one right answer; they are more concerned with flexibility, diversity of expression, and the exploration of alternatives. This requires an approach to teaching that suggests not "this is a . . . ," but instead focuses on "this could be a. . . ." The educational process is one that encourages searching for new answers, not merely for students to give back those answers they have read in a book or heard from an instructor.

Social psychologist Ellen Langer has recommended that this alternative approach be used in a variety of fields and notes the potential results of such an effort: "The key to teaching in this new way is based on an appreciation of both the conditional, or context dependent, nature of the world and the value of uncertainty. Teaching skills and facts in a conditional way sets the stage for doubt and an awareness of how different situations may call for subtle differences in what we bring to them." The result should be more creative and flexible students.

Such an approach, we suggest, makes a good deal of sense for leadership education as well. Leaders operate in a world of constant contingency, that is, very little can be taken as fact, indeed, whatever appears real at one moment is likely soon to be revealed as something that looks a little different. Especially as leaders deal in a world of ethics and values, they face a landscape of shifting sands. Leaders trained to look only for the "right answers" will likely find their training inadequate, even misleading. If you are trained to look for facts you will find facts, or at least things you perceive as factual. If those "facts" are instead contingent, subject to rapid fluctuations and rearrangements, then your perception of them as facts will clearly limit your understanding of what is really going on. In contrast, by coming to view the given world as conditional, potential leaders are probably better equipped to understand, to cope with, and to move change in more positive directions.

The second issue related to arts education but having implications for leadership development has to do with collaboration and mutuality. We mentioned above the participatory nature of the studio experience, that instructors and students come together in the studio to explore together ways in which their artistic work might be improved and their development as creative artists might be enhanced. Obviously, the feedback that comes from one's teachers *and* one's peers is more elaborate, textured, and profound than that from only one individual, the instructor. Having multiple sources of feedback can help the student refine particular works of art or help potential leaders assess their leadership experiences drawn from outside the classroom.

But the process of collaboration also provides students with experiences that go beyond improving individual products or projects and contribute to the development of the individual personality as it engages a world of mutuality. To understand this point, we might start with composer Ernst Krenek's comment that encouraging the student's individual personality, rather than suppressing it, is "one of the vital requirements and the very touchstone of any pedagogical method." Encouraging the individual's personality is not accomplished by imposing ideas from an authority figure, an instructor or the authors of well-known books. Rather, individual development occurs most appropriately through a process of interaction between the individual and others sharing similar interests, in particular an interest in personal development.

What is important about this formulation is that individual development does not occur in a vacuum. Individuals develop their personalities through frequent and multiple interactions with others; indeed, without their interaction with others, and without the sense of mutuality that such interaction implies, artists and leaders would be limited in the resources they are able to bring to bear in realizing their art. Both the artist and the leader must draw from a substantial understanding of the human condition, and education for the art of leadership must provide a contribution to that understanding. Recognizing that one's own development is dependent on others not only contributes to the store of knowledge and experience that leaders possess, it also helps them nurture a larger sense of humanity, something that we think is essential to both art and leadership.

A third issue connecting art education and leadership development has to do with self-reflection and vulnerability. As we have noted, dancers put themselves in a place in which they are extremely open to criticism. Many dancers told us about the vulnerability they feel. Septime Webre, for example, said, "You are never as bare as you are putting your whole body out there. You are exposing your entire self. You are also working in partnerships very intimately with other people, with the most intimate parts of their body, in close contact. There are almost no barriers whatsoever. So the dancers are used to exposing themselves. We are used to showing all of who we are. You can hide behind emotions. You can act. But the mirror is right there. We are forced to be honest with ourselves."

Dancers have to face themselves in a mirror and they are subject to correction after correction. The constant stream of evaluations and suggestions from others would drive most people crazy. Yet dancers have to learn the importance of taking the positive out of even what might seem to be very negative suggestions and to work to improve their art. In part, dancers are aided in this by the fact that the studio experience establishes a norm of openness and safety; it encourages absorption and self-reflection.

Of course, many dancers come to realize that one of the most difficult things for them is to realistically assess themselves as artists. Roy Kaiser of the Pennsylvania Ballet told us, "I talk with dancers all the time and discuss a certain element of their work and they are not even aware of it. They are thinking a completely different way." Dancers learn the importance of seeing themselves as others see them. Interestingly, Kaiser continued by saying, "I've always believed that dancers that are really special are not so aware of that mirror. They are in front of it but it's peripheral. They get past the point of specific technique, but that's not their focus. Their focus is something beyond that. The mirror is a tool but it's not something they focus on." Eventually, of course, the dancer's capacity to endure and eventually to absorb suggestions and corrections is what ultimately leads to the beauty and elegance of the performance.

Leaders don't open themselves to evaluation and criticism in quite the same way as dancers, but leaders at all levels, from the moment they begin to lead, are subject to especially intense evaluation and judgment by others. Of course, at the highest levels of leadership the level of examination and critique is intense. Every little move, as we said earlier, "every little body twitch," is seen as a sign of something important. Whatever the leader does, there are those who disagree and those who second-guess. The leader has to be able to "survive" criticism, to ignore those comments that are mean-spirited but irrelevant, but the leader also has to be able to "take" criticism, in the sense of recognizing and responding to reasonable comments so as to improve his or her capacity to lead.

One thing that those aspiring to leadership often don't recognize, yet one thing the leaders we talked with mentioned over and over, was the fact that leaders don't know everything and often fail. Alan Yordy of PeaceHealth put it this way: "Though there are some 'prodigies' who have a sense of self-assurance, the ability to listen, taking in their environment, synthesizing it into something new and different that makes a world of sense, . . . they are rare. For those of us who aren't that gifted, it takes a lot of experience, it takes having stubbed your toe several times and gotten the black and blue spots from stepping into things." Similarly, when we asked Dan Evans, former governor and senator from Washington, about what leaders learn from experience, he immediately said, "Failure, or at least disappointment. When you start out you think the whole world is going to react marvelously to your great ideas. One of the best things that can happen is to trip and fall and learn from that so you don't trip the next time. If you don't learn from failure then you will fail. If you learn from it you build defenses against the next failure and build successes." We recommend that leadership development includes attention to vulnerability, openness to criticism, and the capacity to learn from one's failures.

We talked earlier about the capacity of leaders to state things in a simple and straightforward way that communicates effectively to others. We thought astronaut Charles Bolden did a marvelous job of doing so when he described a speech he often makes to children. Bolden mentioned three things that he thought were critical, three things, as he said, that "my mom and dad taught me: (1) You've got to study. You've got to equip yourself intellectually so that no matter what comes along you can deal with it. (2) You've got to work very hard. You've got to focus on whatever you are doing at this particular moment. You need to work, work, work on the subject at hand. (3) You cannot be afraid to fail. You've got to be a risk taker. People may say you are out of your mind. But you go out and try. If you fail, that's good because at least you tried. The only way you will turn that failure into success is go back, study hard, and try again."

In other words, you learn, you try, and if you fail you start through the cycle again. Simple words, we would say, but very good advice for potential leaders—or for people generally.

Reprise

Leadership touches the human spirit. Leadership enables us to take that which is ordinary in life and make it extraordinary, to focus not just on the immediate but on the potential that resides within the present. Leadership looks beyond individuals to the relationships that exist among individuals, turning those relationships toward the future so as to provide a hint of what they might become. Leadership takes the energy that connects people, expands it, and turns it into a motive force, compelling people to confront the future with insight and resolve.

Leadership touches the human spirit, and touching the human spirit has always been the work of art and aesthetics. It's not surprising, therefore, that good leaders have always thought of leadership as more of an art than a science. These leaders recognize that leadership means much more than a set of strategies or techniques that might be employed to "get things done." The "science of leadership" can only take us so far. There is a much more mysterious, hard-to-explain aspect of leadership. Yet, as the very best leaders acknowledge, it's this unexplained aspect of leadership, the "art of leadership," that makes all the difference.

In this book we have looked at many different elements of the art of leadership. None of these ideas, however, means anything unless they are put into practice. You ultimately must learn leadership from acting as a leader. "You do not learn to choreograph by reading about it, hearing about it, or by watching major companies in concert. You learn choreography by choreographing, by experimenting, by creating little bits and pieces and fragments of dances and dance phrases, by playing with the materials of the craft over and over again until they become second nature." Similarly, and not surprisingly, you can't learn leadership by reading about it, hearing about, or watching major leaders in action. You learn leadership by leading, by putting yourself "on the line," by assuming the risk and responsibility of leadership, by allowing for the interplay of human emotions and human values that leadership inevitably exposes, and by being fully present and fully committed to the importance of the work. But through care and practice, through empathy and emotion, you can indeed improve your artistry as a leader. You can be a full partner in the dance of leadership.

APPENDIX: LIST OF INTERVIEWEES

Artists, Musicians, and Dancers

Roger Bedard, Department of Theater, Arizona State University
Ron Brown, dancer and choreographer, Ronald K. Brown/Evidence
Joann Browning, dance program, University of Delaware
Cem Catbas, artistic director, Ballet Academy of Baltimore
Elysabeth Catbas, opera singer, Zurich Opera, Prague State Opera
Robert de Warren, artistic director, Sarasota Ballet
Kristina Dippel, principal dancer, First State Ballet
Ellen Dissanyake, independent scholar, aesthetic philosopher
Mary Anne Fernandez-Herding, artistic director, Movement Source
Victoria Hutchinson, dance program, Salisbury State University
Roy Kaiser, artistic director, Pennsylvania Ballet
Pasha Kambalov, artistic director, Russian Ballet Centre
Liz Lerman, artistic director, Liz Lerman Dance Exchange
Andre Lewis, artistic director, Royal Winnipeg Ballet
Donna Maytham, co-founder of the Richmond Ballet
Celeste Miller, dancer and choreographer, Liz Lerman Dance Exchange
Claudia Murphey, Department of Dance, Arizona State University
Matthew Neenan, artistic director and choreographer, Phrenic New Ballet
Tamara Nijinsky and Kinga Gaspers, performance artists, daughter and granddaughter of Vaslav Nijinsky
Vincent Nilsson, internationally known jazz trombonist
Steve Owen, Jazz Studies, University of Oregon
Mila Parrish, Department of Dance, Arizona State University
David Parsons, founder and artistic director, Parsons Dance Company
Carla Perlo, executive/artistic director, Dance Place
Francia Russell, artistic co-director, Pacific Northwest Ballet

Robert Shields, artist and mime (Shields and Yarnell)
Kent Stowell, artistic co-director and choreographer, Pacific Northwest Ballet
Septime Webre, artistic director, Washington Ballet
Betsy Wetzig, movement consultant
John Wilson, professor emeritus, Department of Dance, University of Arizona
Alcine Wiltz, chair, Department of Dance, University of Maryland

Leaders in Business, Government, Nonprofit Organizations, the Military, Higher Education, and the World of Sports

Jemeille Ackourey, Boys and Girls Clubs of America
Louis Blair, executive secretary, Truman Scholarship Foundation
Brig. General Charles Bolden, NASA astronaut and space shuttle commander
Lattie Coor, former president, Arizona State University and University of Vermont
Carole Couture, VP and GMM for CommerceHub; former president, Art Select International
Hugh Downs, legendary broadcaster, host of the *Today Show* and co-anchor of *20/20*
Thomas Downs, former president and CEO, Amtrak
Daniel Evans, former governor and former United States senator, Washington State
George Fisher, retired chairman and CEO, Eastman Kodak, former CEO of Motorola
General Ronald Fogleman, U.S. Air Force retired, former member Joint Chiefs of Staff
David Frohnmayer, president, University of Oregon
Phil Fulmer, head football coach, University of Tennessee
Patti Hall, president and CEO, Helen Ross McNabb Center
Jeanette Harrison, director of knowledge and learning, Intel
Jane Hull, former governor of Arizona
William Jacobs, president, Western Institutional Review Board
Robert Johnson, president and CEO, Honeywell Aerospace
Ernie Kent, head basketball coach, University of Oregon

Catherine McKee, vice-president, General Dynamics Decision Systems

David Miller, Robert Hull, Norm Strong, Craig Curtis, Miller/Hull Partnership

Judy Mohraz, president, Virginia Piper Trust, former president, Goucher College

Larry Newman, entrepreneur, inventor of the ultra-light airplane, and record-setting balloonist

Robert O'Neill, executive director, International City/County Management Association, and former county manager, Fairfax County, Virginia

Jan Perkins, former city manager, Fremont, California

William Post, president and CEO, Pinnacle West

Alan Yordy, president and CEO, PeaceHealth (Oregon)

REFERENCES

By convention, we note without citation where we have drawn quoted material from our interviews.

Chapter 1

8 For example, Max De Pree . . . Max De Pree, *Leadership Jazz* (Currency Doubleday, 1992).

8 "By establishing the theme . . ." Robert B. Denhardt, *The Pursuit of Significance: Strategies for Managerial Success in Public Organizations* (Wadsworth, 1993), pp. 180–181.

9 " Leadership is a . . ." James M. Kouzes and Barry Z. Posner, *The Leadership Challenge,* 3rd ed. (Jossey-Bass, 2002), p. 84.

9 " Artists interpret . . ." Lee G. Bolman and Terrence E. Deal, *Reframing Organizations: Artistry, Choice, and Leadership,* 2nd ed. (Jossey-Bass, 1997), p. 17.

10 The cubist painter . . . Georges Braque, *Illustrated Notebooks, 1917–1955* (Dover Publications, 1971), p. 13.

11 Business executive . . . Chester I. Barnard, *The Functions of the Executive* (Harvard University Press, 1968), p. 235.

11 It is not surprising . . . Quoted in Oren Harari, *The Leadership Secrets of Colin Powell,* 1st ed. (McGraw-Hill, 2002), p. 13. Emphasis added.

13 " We must be . . ." Constance A. Schrader, *A Sense of Dance: Exploring Your Movement Potential* (Human Kinetics, 1996), p. 14.

13 But, the irony is . . . Lynne Anne Blom and L. Tarin Chaplin, *The Intimate Act of Choreography* (University of Pittsburgh Press, 1982), p. 201.

13 " Life only lasts . . ." Walter Sorell, *The Dancer's Image: Points & Counterpoints* (Columbia University Press, 1971), p. 11.

16 As one critic . . . Ellen Dissanayake, *Art and Intimacy: How the Arts Began* (University of Washington Press, 2000), p. 204.

21 "A dance . . ." Suzanne Langer, quoted in Joan Cass, *The Dance* (McFarland & Co., 1999), p. 4.

Chapter 2

25 "The value of . . ." Barbara Schaffer Bacon, Cheryl Yuen, and Pam Korza, "Animating Democracy," *Americans for the Arts,* 1999, p. 12.

30 "The mime must . . ." Quoted in Keith Johnstone, *Impro: Improvisation and the Theatre* (Theatre Arts Books, 1979), p. 55.

32 " There are certain . . ." Silvano Arieti, *Creativity: The Magic Synthesis* (Basic Books, 1976), p. 377.
39 " The arts give . . . " Dissanayake, *Art and Intimacy*, p. 196.
40 The master of . . . Rudolf von Laban and Lisa Ullmann, *The Mastery of Movement,* 3rd ed. (Macdonald & Evans, 1971), p. 19.
41 "What inner impulse . . . " Schrader, *A Sense of Dance*, p. 90.
41 "Dance provides something . . ." Quoted in Maxine Sheets-Johnstone, *Illuminating Dance: Philosophical Explorations* (Bucknell University Press, 1984), p. 40.
41 " I'm very excited . . ." Quoted in Jim Taylor and Ceci Taylor, *The Psychology of Dance* (Human Kinetics, 1995), p. 120.
42 "The person who . . . " Quoted in Blom and Chaplin, *The Intimate Act of Choreography*, p. 14.
43 "Any work of art . . ." Margaret Newell H'Doubler, *Dance: A Creative Art Experience* (F.S. Crofts and Company, 1940), p. 103.
43 "It articulates who . . ." George Hagman quoted in Carol M. Press, *The Dancing Self* (Hampton Press, 2002), p. 204.
44 Certainly dancers think . . . Blom and Chaplin, 1982, p. 7.
44 "Having studied . . ." Marshall Dimock, "Creativity," *Public Administration Review* 46, no. 1 (1986): p. 6.

Chapter 3

49 To say that something . . . Francis Sparshott, *A Measured Pace* (University of Toronto Press, 1995), p. 160.
50 "The joyous beat . . . " Havelock Ellis, *The Dance of Life* (Houghton Mifflin Company, 1923), p. 36.
51 Some have even . . . Dissanayake, *Art and Intimacy,* William Hardy McNeill, *Keeping Together in Time* (Harvard University Press, 1995).
51 They become means . . . Dissanayake, *Art and Intimacy,* p. 139.
52 It may even . . . McNeill, *Keeping Together in Time,* p. 7.
53 "The rhythms of . . ." H'Doubler, *Dance,* p. 7.
54 "In relation to . . ." Ibid., p. 87.
56 But at the end . . . Daniel Goleman, Richard E. Boyatzis, and Annie McKee, *Primal Leadership* (Harvard Business School Press, 2002), p. 7.
56 "Matching or imitating . . . " Dissanayake, *Art and Intimacy,* p. 40.
56 "He realized that . . . " Edward Hall, *The Dance of Life* (Anchor Press/Doubleday, 1983), p. 55.
57 The reason for this . . . Doris Humphrey, *The Art of Making Dances* (Rinehart, 1959), p. 104.
58 Similarly, social scientists . . . McNeill, *Keeping Together in Time*, p. 156.
58 In their characterizations . . . Frank A. Dubinskas, "Janus Organizations," in *Making Time,* ed. Frank A. Dubinskas, pp. 170–232 (Temple University Press, 1988), p. 201.
58 As H'Doubler wrote . . . Margaret Newell H'Doubler and Elna Mygdal, *Rhythmic Form and Analysis* (J.M. Rider, 1932), p. 4.
62 "When people or . . ." James Jones, "Cultural Differences in Temporal Perspectives," in *The Social Psychology of Time,* pp. 21–38, ed. Joseph Edward McGrath (Sage Publications, 1988), p. 24.

64 "Cycles may repeat . . ." Deborah Ancona and Chee-Leong Chong, "Entrainment: Pace, Cycle, and Rhythm in Organizational Behavior," *Research in Organizational Behavior* 18 (1996), p. 258.
64 For example, in one hospital . . . Ibid., p. 261.
64 For example, consider . . . Allen C. Bluedorn, *The Human Organization of Time* (Stanford Business Books, 2002), pp. 146–147.
66 "Discovering how to . . ." Paul Taylor, *Private Domain* (Knopf, 1987), p. 77.
70 "A steady rhythm . . ." Ellen Dissanayake, *Homo Aestheticus* (University of Washington Press, 1995), p. 83.
74 In a rational . . . Stuart Albert, "Towards a Theory of Timing." *Research in Organizational Behavior* 17 (1995), p. 20.
76 The philosopher . . . Suzanne Langer and Gary Van Den Heuvel, *Mind* (Johns Hopkins University Press, 1988), p. 80.
76 Rhythm is . . . Ibid., p. 80.
76 "All movement on earth is governed ..." Quoted in Roger Copeland and Marshall Cohen, *What Is Dance?* (Oxford University Press, 1983).

Chapter 4

81 Philosopher Joan Cass . . . Cass, *The Dance*, p. 5.
81 "I mean that . . . " Quoted in Dissanayake, *Homo Aestheticus,* p. 166.
82 "To be sure . . ." Rudolf Arnheim, *The Split and the Structure* (University of California Press, 1996), p. 93.
82 "It does not matter . . ." Sorrell, *The Dancer's Image,* p. 16.
83 While this view . . . Howard Gardner, *Frames of Mind* (Basic Books, 1983).
83 More recently . . . Daniel Goleman, *Emotional Intelligence* (Bantam Books, 1995), p. 40.
83 In the book . . . Goleman, Boyatzis, and McKee, *Primal Leadership,* p. 3.
86 In Carl Rogers's . . . Carl R. Rogers, *On Becoming a Person* (Houghton Mifflin, 1951), p. 137.
87 "This means . . ." John Reed Hodgson and Ernest Richards, *Improvisation* (Methuen, 1966), p. 22.
92 Martha Graham . . . Quoted in Roger Copeland and Marshall Cohen, *What Is Dance?* (Oxford University Press, 1983), p. 200.
92 As dance educators . . . Blom and Chaplin, *The Intimate Act of Choreography,* p. 204.
93 Albert Einstein said . . . Quoted in Dimock, "Creativity," p. 1.
95 As this can be . . . Quoted in Schrader, *A Sense of Dance*, p. 161.
96 In their book . . . Gail T. Fairhurst and Robert A. Sarr, *The Art of Framing* (Jossey-Bass Publishers, 1996).
96 Fairhurst and Sarr advise . . . Ibid., p. 172.
98 "I have watched . . . " Quoted in Patricia C. Pitcher, *The Drama of Leadership* (John Wiley, 1997), p. 24.
98 Leaders often use . . . Jay A. Conger, *Winning 'em Over* (Simon & Schuster, 1998).
98 "Leaders who use . . ." Cynthia G. Emrich, Holly H. Brower, Jack M. Feldman, and Howard Garland, "Images in Words: Presidential Rhetoric, Charisma, and Greatness," *Administrative Science Quarterly* 46 (2001): p. 529.

102 "The human body . . ." Quoted in Jean Morrison Brown, Naomi Mindlin, and Charles Humphrey Woodford, *The Vision of Modern Dance,* 2nd ed. (Princeton Book Co., 1997), p. 100.
104 "Movement is the . . ." Blom and Chaplin, *Intimate Act,* p. 6.
105 According to Constance Schrader . . . Schrader, *A Sense of Dance,* p. 22.

Chapter 5

109 When he was told . . . Mildred Portney Chase, *Improvisation* (Creative Arts Book Co., 1988), p. 97.
111 In fact . . . Johnstone, *Impro,* p. 78.
111 Pablo Picasso . . . Quoted in Daniel Nagrin, *Choreography and the Specific Image* (University of Pittsburgh Press, 2001), p. 158.
113 "Leadership is . . . " Ronald Heifetz and Marty Linsky, *Leadership on the Line* (Harvard Business School Press, 2002), p. 73.
114 And, as we . . . Rosabeth Moss Kantor, "Strategy as Improvisational Theatre," *Sloan Management Review.* 43, no. 2 (Winter 2002): pp. 76–81.
114 As jazz musician . . . Quoted in Marquette Folley-Cooper, Deborah Macanic, Janice McNeil, Elizabeth Goldson, and Smithsonian Institution, Traveling Exhibition Service, *Seeing Jazz* (Chronicle Books in association with Smithsonian Institution Traveling Exhibition Service, 1997), p. 65.
115 " An ability to . . ." Derek Bailey, *Improvisation: Its Nature and Practice in Music* (The British Library, 1992), p. 12.
115 "Even improvisation groups . . ." M.M. Crossan, "The Improvising Organization: Where Planning Meets Opportunity," *Organizational Dynamics* 24, no. 4 (1996): p. 34.
116 For these planned . . . Chase, *Improvisation,* p. 30.
116 But the strength . . . Susan Fitzpatrick, "The Imaginary and Improvisation in Public Administration," *Administrative Theory and Praxis* (2002): p. 643.
118 As art philosopher . . . R.G. Collingwood and Alan Donagan, *Essays in the Philosophy of Art* (Indiana University Press, 1964), p. 202.
122 "You go back . . ." Charles Palus and David Horth, *The Leaders Edge* (Jossey-Bass, 2002), p. 73.
123 "To improvise is . . ." John Corbett, "Ephemera Underscored: Writing Around Free Improvisation," in *Jazz among the Discourses,* ed. Krin Gabbard (Duke University Press, 1995), p. 222.
125 Dancer and teacher . . . Press, *The Dancing Self,* p. 176.
126 As choreographer . . . Taylor, *Private Domain,* p. 288.
126 "I began to . . ." Quoted in Taylor and Taylor, *The Psychology of Dance,* p. 50.
126 Drummer and pianist . . . Jack DeJohnette, *Down Beat,* May 1998.
126 "It doesn't only . . ." Derek Bailey, *Improvisation* (Da Capo Press, 1993), p. 49.
130 Jazz flutist David Williams . . . Quoted in Krin Gabbard, ed., *Representing Jazz* (Duke University Press, 1995), p. 225.
130 In the world . . . Andre Lepecki, "The Liberation of Space," *Ballet International,* no. 2 (1997): 14–19.
131 "The Improv itself . . ." Robert Lowe, *Improvisation, Inc.* (Jossey-Bass/Pfeiffer, 2000), p. 31.

Chapter 6

135 As choreographer . . . Quoted in Phillip G. Clampitt and Robert J. Dekoch, *Embracing Uncertainty* (M.E. Sharpe, 2001), p. 199.
140 Martha Graham stated . . . Quoted in Taylor and Taylor, *The Psychology of Dance,* p. 71.
141 Yogi Berra also . . . Quoted in Schrader, *A Sense of Dance,* p. 105.
141 "There is a time . . ." Taylor and Taylor, *The Psychology of Dance,* p. 46.
145 "It's a certain . . ." Quoted in Bailey, *Improvisation,* p. 52.
146 Agnes de Mille . . . Quoted in Taylor and Taylor, 1995, p. 22.
146 Dancer and experimentalist . . . Quoted in Ellen Switzer, *Dancers!* (Atheneum, 1982), p. 261.
147 "Nobody is born . . ." Quoted in ibid., p. 209.
147 Choreographer George Balanchine . . . Quoted in ibid., p. 129.
147 "I also had . . . Quoted in Taylor and Taylor, 1995, p. 20.
151 "The dancer with . . ." Quoted in Taylor and Taylor, 1995, p. 37.
151 "Dancers can influence . . ." Taylor and Taylor, 1995, p. 41.
156 A dance seeks . . . Blom and Chaplin, *The Intimate Act of Choreography,* p. 30.
156 Similarly, for individuals . . . Peter B. Vaill, *Managing as a Performing Art* (Jossey-Bass, 1989), p. 121.
158 Dancer and choreographer Daniel Nagrin . . . Nagrin, *Choreography and the Specific Image,* p. 40.
158 Dancer and choreographer Charles Weidman . . . Quoted in Brown, Mindlin, and Woodford, *The Vision of Modern Dance*, p. 67.
159 "Dance generates . . ." Randy Martin, *Critical Moves* (Duke University Press, 1998), p. 1.
159 "All movement can . . ." Quoted in Brown, Mindlin, and Woodford, *The Vision of Modern Dance*, p. 60.
160 "The artist creates . . ." Sorell, *The Dancer's Image*, pp. 4–5.
160 We need not . . . Edward Hirsch, *The Demon and the Angel* (Harcourt, 2002).
262 "If someone choreographs . . ." Quoted in Press, *The Dancing Self,* p. 35.

Chapter 7

171 "The key to . . ." Quoted in Phillip G. Clampitt and Robert J. DeKoch, *Embracing Uncertainty* (M.E. Sharpe, 2002), p. 18.
172 To understand this . . . Quoted in Chase, *Improvisation,* p. 60.
175 "You do not . . ." Blom and Chaplin, *The Intimate Act of Choreography,* p. 3.

INDEX

Robert B. Denhardt is Lincoln Professor of Leadership and Ethics, Director of the School of Public Affairs at Arizona State University, and Visiting Scholar at the University of Delaware. Dr. Denhardt is a past president of the American Society for Public Administration and a member of the National Academy of Public Administration. He has published seventeen books, including *The New Public Service, Managing Human Behavior in Public and Non-Profit Organizations, Theories of Public Organization, Public Administration: An Action Orientation, In the Shadow of Organization, The Pursuit of Significance, Executive Leadership in the Public Service, The Revitalization of the Public Service,* and *Pollution and Public Policy.*

Janet V. Denhardt is Professor of Public Administration in the School of Public Affairs at Arizona State University. Dr. Denhardt has authored three books: *The New Public Service, Managing Human Behavior in Public and Nonprofit Organizations, and Street-Level Leadership,* and *Public Administration: An Action Orientation.* She has also published more than two dozen monographs, chapters, and articles in journals, including the *Public Administration Review, Administration & Society,* and the *American Review of Public Administration.*

A Leadership Development Workshop

Managers and leaders recognize that leadership is more of an art than a science. *The Dance of Leadership Workshop* focuses on the *art* of leadership, employing material from art, music, and especially dance to discover new ways of thinking about leadership and new ways of sharpening one's leadership skills. For anyone who wants to lead, whether in a small group, a community, a public, private, or non-profit organization, *The Dance of Leadership Workshop* will provide special insight and understanding of the art of leading others to achieve shared goals.

The Dance of Leadership Workshop is a multi-media presentation, highly interactive, and best suited to groups of twenty to fifty meeting for either a three hour period or larger groups meeting for a one and a half hour period. It involves brief lecturettes, conversations, and demonstrations through art, music, and dance (though don't worry, no dancing is required!).

The Presenter—An internationally known educator and motivational speaker, Robert B. Denhardt is a member of the faculty at Arizona State University. He is a past National President of the American Society for Public Administration and the author of seventeen books on management, leadership, and organizational change.